Series / Number 07-036

ACHIEVEMENT TESTING
Recent Advances

ISAAC I. BEJAR
Educational Testing Service

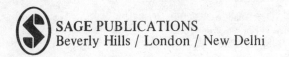

SAGE PUBLICATIONS
Beverly Hills / London / New Delhi

For information address:

SAGE Publications, Inc.
275 South Beverly Drive
Beverly Hills, California 90212

SAGE Publications Inc.
2111 West Hillcrest Drive
Newbury Park
California 91320

SAGE Publications Ltd.
28 Banner Street
London EC1Y 8QE
England

SAGE PUBLICATIONS India Pvt. Ltd.
M-32 Market
Greater Kailash I
New Delhi 110 048 India

International Standard Book Number 0-8039-2047-4

Library of Congress Catalog Card No. 83-050514

SECOND PRINTING

When citing a university paper, please use the proper form. Remember to cite the correct
Sage University Paper series title and include the paper number. One of the following
formats can be adapted (depending on the style manual used):

(1) IVERSEN, GUDMUND R. and NORPOTH, HELMUT (1976) "Analysis of
Variance." Sage University Paper series on Quantitative Applications in the Social
Sciences, 07-001. Beverly Hills: Sage Pubns.

OR

(2) Iversen, Gudmund R. and Norpoth, Helmut. 1976. *Analysis of Variance.* Sage
University Paper series on Quantitative Applications in the Social Sciences, series no.
07-001. Beverly Hills: Sage Pubns.

CONTENTS

Series Editor's Introduction

Dr. Isaac Bejar reviews recent developments in achievement testing. Since he is associated with Educational Testing Service, he is in the forefront of the field and is in a position to remain abreast of newer work on achievement testing even before it finds its way into the academic journals. Dr. Bejar makes good use of this vantage point in writing *Achievement Testing*.

This monograph represents something of a departure from our usual topics in this series. It is somewhat more specialized, being on achievement testing rather than on the broader topic of tests and measurement. We fully intend to publish additional manuscripts covering other aspects of psychological and educational testing. This paper is also a departure in that it is a review of recent developments rather than a technical presentation designed to be a sort of primer or introduction to some aspect of quantitative methodology. Dr. Bejar uses very few equations in his presentation. Rather, he provides an overview of many different aspects of achievement testing and tries to bring the reader up to date in the field. As a result, the reader should have some basic familiarity with analysis of variance (see the first paper, by Iversen and Norpoth, in this series) and with educational testing (see also Osterlind, 1983) in order to fully understand the arguments presented by Dr. Bejar.

Achievement Testing discusses the psychometric foundations of test theory, including the basic outlines of the random sampling (R-S) model and its major competitor, the latent trait (L-T) model. The former assumes that items are sampled at random from a universe of items, whereas the latter assumes that there is a specific relationship between an item and the level of achievement. Dr. Bejar provides some historical background on these two models and discusses their application to achievement testing. He discusses briefly the problems of statistical estimation and item analysis, as well as the assumptions underlying the two models. He then presents a very cogent section comparing the two models in terms of achievement testing.

In addition to discussing the psychometric foundations of achievement testing, Dr. Bejar covers administration procedures, including recent developments in computer-assisted adaptive testing and varying approaches to the interpretation of achievement test scores. In the case of the latter, he pays particular attention to the differences between norm-referenced testing and criterion-referenced testing. He concludes the manuscript with a discussion of the future of achievement testing.

We are delighted to add *Achievement Testing* to our list of offerings. We believe it will be a valuable addition to the professional libraries of educational testing specialists and psychometricians.

—*John L. Sullivan*
Series Co-Editor

ACHIEVEMENT TESTING
Recent Advances

ISAAC I. BEJAR
Educational Testing Service

1. INTRODUCTION

These days it is not easy to be a psychometrician. Tests are continually under attack by various constituencies, and not a single cocktail party goes by without someone making an unkind remark about testing and those associated with it. As uncomfortable as this situation can be, such criticisms are useful in that they motivate research, which in the end improves the state of the art. For example, when the truth-in-testing legislation was approved, there was significant increase in research activity related to the problem of equating test scores under the new set of administration constraints. Even in the absence of legislation, the testing field has been responsive to new concerns. This is reflected, for example, in the incorporation of ethics as an integral part of the validation of tests (Messick, 1980) as well as in the creative incorporation of technology both in the test development process (Roid and Haladyna, 1982) and the test administration process (e.g., Weiss, 1982).

The purpose of this paper is to chronicle some of these developments —as succintly as possible—as they apply to achievement, in contrast to "ability," tests, although to be sure many of the recent developments are equally applicable to both achievement and ability testing. The framework in which I have chosen to report these developments is to view achievement testing as a system with several interrelated components to be described below. This approach will be welcomed by those consider-

AUTHOR'S NOTE: This work was supported in part by contract NR150-389 with the Office of Naval Research—David J. Weiss, principal investigator. I would like to express appreciation for the comments and suggestions of Ron Hambleton and Bob Brennan on an earlier version of the manuscript.

ing the establishment of a "state-of-the-art" achievement testing program, as well as by those who may want to have a better understanding of what those components are and how they interrelate.

Overview

A foremost consideration in designing and constructing an achievement testing system is conceptualizing and creating a conglomerate of items from which tests can eventually be put together. The conventional procedure for developing items has been to use item writers, which naturally introduces a subjective component into the process. Developments in recent years have, however, made it possible to eliminate that subjective component by generating items according to algorithms. The next section reviews some of these procedures.

The psychometric foundation of an achievement testing system also requires careful consideration. Two major theories serve that purpose. One is based on the assumption that items can be sampled at random from a "universe" of items. A common objection to this theory involves questioning the implementability of this fundamental assumption (Loevinger, 1965). Nevertheless, the algorithms for item generation, mentioned in the preceding paragraph, would appear to make this approach feasible. The second measurement model does not make any assumptions about the sampling of items, but instead assumes that the relationship between observed performance and level of achievement is known or can be estimated.

These two models, which will be referred to as the R-S (random sampling) model and the L-T (latent trait) model, make different explicit assumptions. I shall identify and discuss these assumptions, contrast the capabilities of the two models, and evaluate their applicability to achievement testing.

A third component of an achievement testing system is the administration procedure. For the last several decades, paper-and-pencil group administrators have been standard in achievement testing. Because of advances in both psychometrics and computer technology, tailoring the test to the individual has become possible, with and without computers. In the third section I shall review the applicability of this new technology to achievement testing.

Once the administration has taken place, the user must face the problem both of understanding what the test scores mean and of eventually making instructional decisions based on those scores. These problems have dominated discussions about achievement testing, as evidenced by the continuing debate over the concepts of criterion-referenced and norm-referenced tests. It is concluded that neither criterion-referenced nor norm-referenced interpretations of achievement scores are sufficient, since neither type of interpretation does justice to the dynamic nature of achievement. I argue, therefore, that new validation procedures are required. Some of the possibilities open to us will be discussed.

In the last section I discuss the adequacy of existing models and procedures in view of technological advances and changing social expectations about the role of measurement in education.

2. CONCEPTUALIZING AND CREATING THE UNIVERSE OF ITEMS

A logical prerequisite to the generation of items is conceptualizing them in terms of the instructional program. Shoemaker (1975), for example, has argued that there must be an isomorphism between the instructional program and the items associated with it. That is, the knowledge required to answer every item must be obtainable through instruction. The insistence that *every* item be answerable as a result of instruction has naturally led to the notion of a "universe" of items. To define such a universe, it is necessary first to identify all its constituent elements. That task, however, is practically impossible to achieve by traditional procedures of item generation, in which each item is painstakingly edited until it reaches its final version. The enumeration of the universe of items is now possible, in principle, because of an exciting development—the invention of item-writing algorithms. This development is important not only because it has implications for item generation, but also because it permits the realization of the key assumption of the R-S model, namely, sampling items from a universe of items.

The next section briefly describes how items are usually written and discusses some of the algorithms that have been suggested for item generation.

The Traditional Approach

In a chapter on the traditional approach to generating an item pool for standardized achievement tests, Wessman (1971) termed the process a creative one. He listed as qualifications of item writers a "well developed set of educational values" and an understanding of the individuals for whom the test is intended. In his description it is up to the item writer to produce items that satisfy the specifications of the test plan:

> Item writing is essentially creative—it is an art. Just as there can be no set of formulas for producing a good story or a good painting, so there can be no set of rules that guarantees the production of good test items. Principles can be established and suggestions offered, but it is the item writer's judgment in the application—and occasional disregard—of these principles and suggestions that determines whether good items or mediocre ones are produced. Each item, as it is being written, presents new problems and new opportunities. Thus, item writing requires an uncommon combination of special abilities and is mastered only through extensive and critically supervised practice [Wessman, 1971: 81].

This description suggests that, although the process is not haphazard, it is certainly idiosyncratic, since it is largely the item writer's responsibility to interpret what is wanted and to generate items that meet the prescription.

Nothing in that description suggests how to ensure that a given item will measure achievement in a particular domain. Presumably, a good item writer will do this precisely because he or she is a good item writer. Similarly, a good item writer should be able to evaluate the work of other item writers. Unfortunately, we are left without any explicit guidelines for generating and evaluating pertinent items.

Guttman's Facet Approach

Guttman and his associates have suggested procedures to systematize the generation of items (Guttman and Schlesinger, 1967) while still relying on item writers. The approach requires that the facets or content categories of the achievement domains and the facets of the possible responses be clearly spelled out. However, as Millman (1974) has pointed out, not all the ambiguities inherent in item writing are eliminated by this approach. Nevertheless, facet analysis may be viewed as a general framework under which several specific models can be accommodated. For example Guilford's (1959) model of intellect can be viewed as a delineation of the facets of intelligent behaviors, in which the content facets constitute the "input," the operation facets constitute "processing," and the product facets constitute "output" or responses. A similar model may be postulated for achievement, as Gagné (1975) has done. (See also Berk, 1978.)

According to Guttman and Schlesinger (1967), the benefits of the facet approach include the possibility of writing distractors with varying degrees of attractiveness or distractors representing different types of errors. This possibility would enable the implementation of differential option-weighting schemes. Although the empirical literature has not convincingly demonstrated the usefulness of differential option weighting (Wang and Stanley, 1970; Wood, 1976), it is also true that most studies have used items for which no attempt has been made to construct distractors of differential attractiveness. Theoretical investigations (e.g., Bejar and Weiss, 1977), on the other hand, have shown that great gains in validity and reliability can be expected as a result of differential option weighting when distractors differ in attractiveness.

Although Guttman himself shuns cognitive interpretations of test performance, the facet approach lends itself well to such interpretations. Feldman and Markwalder (1971), for example, constructed a map-reading test in which the distractors within each item would be attractive to children at different stages of cognitive development. They found that, by and large, children responded in accordance with Piaget's model of cognitive development.

In sum, the facet approach requires careful thought on the part of the test developer. For this, if for no other reason, its implementation in a testing program is likely to have a salutary effect on test quality.

Linguistic-Based Approach

Among the critics of the traditional item-generation practices, Bormuth (1970) has perhaps reacted most forcefully. In his view, traditionally constructed achievement tests are not capable of addressing the kinds of questions for which they are used. He has identified at least four problems with the traditional approach.

(1) The phrasing of the item is left to the item writer.
(2) The closeness with which the item taps the intended behavior is left entirely to the item writer.
(3) Item writers write only items that they think are right; i.e., they avoid items that are trivial, too complex, too simple, or too wordy.
(4) Items produced in the traditional fashion do not necessarily have a logical relation to instruction.

Bormuth views these problems as sufficient reasons to reject the traditional approach. He has suggested as a solution the algorithmization of the item-generating process. His suggestion can be implemented if it is possible to represent the instructional program by a finite set of sentences; then, by means of item transformations on those sentences, the item universe can be generated in principle.

The item transformation referred to above is a linguistic operation performed on a statement of an instructional program. To be useful, such transformations must be capable of generating populations of items: "To be specific, a given set of operations should be capable of being systematically applied to an instructional program in such a way that all the items of the type derivable by those operations will be produced" (Bormuth, 1970: 35).

Several kinds of transformation have been developed; for the most part, however, they can be applied to instructional programs that can be stated in natural language (Bormuth, 1970: 39). As a simple example consider the sentence, "The weather is warm." By performing transformations on this sentence, items may be derived. A simple transformation that results in an "echo question" consists simply of changing the period to a question mark. The item derived from this transformation is "The weather is warm?" Other transformations can be applied as well to generate items such as the following:

- "Is the weather warm?" (yes/no item)
- "The weather is warm, is it not?" (tag items)

While the conceptual beauty of Bormuth's system is widely recognized (e.g., Cronbach, 1970), it is not an understatement to say that the approach has seldom been applied. Bormuth was the first to recognize the limitations of his method, including the possibility of generating trivial or grammatically unacceptable items.

Improvements over the original formulation, suggested by Finn (1975, 1978), seem to avoid some of the difficulties. It is important to note that in Finn's approach, item writers are involved in the process of generating the items, but their judgment is guided by Finn's algorithm. Even when all the technical difficulties are resolved, however, the applicability of this method seems limited to instructional programs the content of which can be explicitly described with a set of finite, natural-language sentences. Its usefulness, therefore, may be limited (Shoemaker, 1975), but there are some practical alternatives.

ITEM FORMS

The proponents of the item-form approach (Osburn, 1968; Hively, 1974) were motivated, as Bormuth was, to suggest alternative testing

ITEM FORM SHELL

DIRECTIONS:	SCRIPT:
Read script to child:	Tell me a number that is _____(a)_____
Write down child's exact words.	

CELL MATRIX

	1	2	3	4
Script (a)	"greater than (b_1)"	"less than (b_1)"	"greater than (b_1) but less than (b_2)"	
Numerals (b)	$0 \leq b_1 \leq 19$	$1 \leq b_1 \leq 20$	$0 \leq b_1 \leq 18$ and $(b_1 + 2) \leq b_2 \leq 20$	$0 \leq b_1 \leq 19$ and $b_2 = b_1 + 1$

SOURCE: W. Hively, "Introduction to Domain Referenced Testing," *Educational Technology,* Vol. 14, pp. 5-9. Copyright © 1974 by Educational Technology Publications, Inc. Reprinted by permission.

Example 1 Examples of an Item Form

schemes because of their dissatisfaction with the traditional approach to writing achievement items. Osburn (1968) argued that the arbitrary way in which items are selected for inclusion in an achievement test prevents the formation of an empirical basis for generalizing beyond what occurs on a specific test. To achieve generalization it is necessary to create an item universe that better represents the instructional material (Hively, 1974: 6). One way to generate such a universe is through an "item form," which Hively defined as a list of rules for generating a set of items. An item, in turn, is defined as a "set of instructions telling how to evoke, detect and score a specific bit of human performance. It must include directions for (1) presenting the stimuli, (2) recording the response, and (3) deciding whether or not the response is appropriate" (Hively, 1974: 8).

The item form consists of two parts: a "shell" (i.e., a set of instructions for administering and scoring) and the stem or question itself. The following example is taken from Hively (1974). By substituting the three possible scripts, three kinds of items are generated. By inserting specific numerals into the script, we can then generate the population of items, although in practice it is not necessary to do so. That is, one can sample at random from the universe defined by that item form without ever having to enumerate all the items.

Scandura's Structural Approach

Scandura (1977) has proposed not so much an algorithm for generating an item pool, but an entire performance test theory that links instructional and measurement considerations in a unified scheme for achievement testing. His proposal has distinct implications for defining the item pool and constructing items for it. Like other critics of conventional testing, Scandura has argued that test results should indicate the specific capabilities of an individual by relating his or her performance on the test to an objective criterion. He has also argued that it is not sufficient to describe the behaviors a student is able to perform; it is also necessary to specify what the learner must know in order to perform those behaviors successfully. In his terminology, the "rules of competence"—the processes that collectively make it possible to solve a problem—must be defined as well. This view of achievement testing contrasts sharply with the view held by advocates of mastery testing (e.g., Block, 1971). In mastery testing the exclusive concern is whether the student is able to perform successfully on an agreed-upon proportion of items from the universe. The proportion must, in the absence of a theory of instruction, be judgmentally determined. The advantage of Scandura's approach is that by specifying the rules of competence, one simultaneously determines the rules for generating items. If one examines performance on items calling for certain rules of competence, it is possible to determine what the individual has learned and what remains to be learned. An added benefit of Scandura's approach is that the rules of competence are also the instructional objectives; thereby the match between instruction and the item universe is facilitated.

To comprehend Scandura's approach, consider the problem of measuring skill in subtraction. The theory behind this skill (i.e., the rules of competence) are found in Example 2. The diagram serves not only as a theory of the subtracting process but also tells the instructor what to teach and the tester what to test. The diamond-shaped figures define kinds of items that call for increasingly more complex rules of competence. Performance on items calling for the indicated rule of competence is expected to be perfect if individuals have mastered that rule. Thus, to

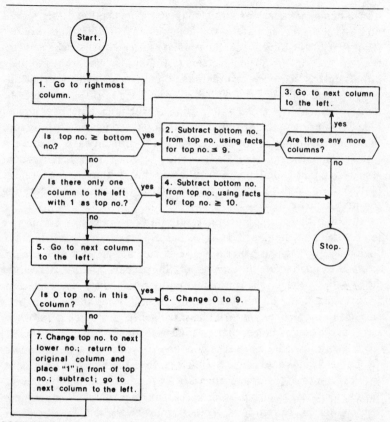

SOURCE: J.M. Scandura, "Structural Approach to Instructional Problems," *American Psychologist*, Vol. 32, pp. 33-53. Copyright © 1977 by American Psychological Association. Reprinted by permission.

Example 2 Rules of Competence for Subtraction

fully describe an individual's level of skill in subtraction, it would be necessary to examine his or her performance on items calling for each of the component rules of competence.

Summary and Evaluation

One of the most significant developments in achievement testing in recent years has been a movement against the traditional approach of "writing" items. The alternative procedures that have been suggested have several related rationales. One of these is to standardize the generation of items so that performance on them can be maximally dependent on instruction. To the extent that item-generation algorithms produce items that give an improved indication of a testee's level of achievement, their integration into an achievement testing system would be extremely important. As yet, however, there is no convincing evidence that this improvement has occurred. Haladyna and Roid (1978) compared the items generated by an item writer using instructional objectives and an item writer using the algorithmic approach. They reported no difference in the instructional sensitivity (i.e., change in difficulty as a function of instruction) of items generated by either approach. In a subsequent study Roid and Haladyna (1978) showed that, within the algorithmic approach, some strategies are more effective than others in generating sensitive items.

Although these experimental results are encouraging, it must be emphasized that item writers were used. This means that what the linguistic approach to generating items can do, at least in the near future, is to standardize the item-generating process. There is, of course, the possibility that in the future a computer could be programmed to perform that task. Bejar (forthcoming b and c) has speculated that, through techiques used in artificial intelligence, it may be possible to tease out the factors that account for the psychometric characteristics of items. This knowledge can be used, in turn, to synthesize items of known psychometric characteristics. Such research is not likely to yield con-crete outcomes in the near future. In the meantime, generating items through the conventional procedure is a viable alternative. The problem pointed out by Bormuth and others may be viewed as sources of measurement errors. Though it is admirable to strive for perfection, not achieving it is no reason to discard all our efforts. In fact, at least in the behavioral sciences, theories and models that cannot stand the presence of error are themselves doomed to failure.

The importance of item-generating algorithms lies primarily in the increased attention they give to obtaining a better match between assessment and instruction (Roid and Haladyna, 1980). The spirit behind these algorithms should be kept in mind whenever an item pool is being created. This spirit seems to have been present in the implementa-tion of item banking by Wood and Skurnik (1969). Even though items were produced by item writers, utmost attention was given to content as well. The writers collected and produced items according to "blueprints" agreed upon beforehand by the eventual users of the pool. It is interest-ing to note that the envisioned purpose of developing the item bank was to allow localities to design their own tests, which would presumably be based on what had actually been taught in that locality. This, it seems, is another way of striving toward the ideal of having performance depend maximally on exposure to instruction. However, the idea of selecting items from a bank or pool rather than sampling them at random raises issues of a psychometric nature that we will turn to in the following section.

3. PSYCHOMETRIC FOUNDATIONS

Once the item pool is available, the problem of describing the characteristics of those items must be confronted and assumptions made as to how students respond to those items. It is at this stage that a bifurcation in approaches to achievement measurement begins to be clearly perceived. There are basically two fully developed test theories that may serve as the psychometric framework for achievement testing. One of these is based on the notion that items are sampled at random from a universe, but no explicit assumptions are made about the stochastic process that generates a response. This approach will be referred to as the random sampling (R-S) model. Its mathematical rationale is found most fully stated in Cronbach et al. (1972) and Brennan (1983; see also Lord and Novick, 1968: chap. 11). The second approach does not make an assumption about the sampling of items from a universe. Instead, it makes an explicit assumption about the relationship between performance on an item and level of achievement. This approach will be referred to as the latent trait (L-T) model. The development of this approach is found in Lord and Novick (1968), Birnbaum (1968), and Lord (1980a).

It should be emphasized that classical test theory (Gulliksen, 1950) is not included under the L-T model. In classical test theory it is not assumed that items are chosen at random, nor is an explicit assumption made as to the relationship between performance and level of achievement. Instead, it is assumed that parallel forms of a test can be constructed. The difficulties with the classical model were noted as early as Guttman's (1953) review of Gulliksen's book. Basically, Guttman objected to the notion of parallel forms because it was conceivable for a test to have several reliabilities. As it turned out, this was not the real difficulty, since, in the broader context of generalizability theory, it is appropriate for a test to have more than one "reliability." The real problem was that classical test theory, by virtue of being a special case of generalizability theory in which items are fixed rather than sampled from a universe, could not accommodate the notion that a test had more than one reliability.

Brief Historical Background

The distinction between the R-S and L-T models appears to have first been drawn by Tryon (1957), who criticized psychometricians for having "clung either to the orthodox theory of true and error factors or to the theory of equivalent test samples—the first a set of unverified postulates, the second obviously unrealistic" (Tryon, 1957: 244). He distinguished between three theories: the true-and-error-factor theory, which is a very primitive L-T model; the theory of equivalent samples, which we have called the classical model; and a theory based on random sampling from a universe.

The distinction between these two approaches was rekindled by Osburn (1968) in an influential paper.

> Few measurement specialists would quarrel with the premise that the fundamental objective of achievement testing in generalization. Yet the fact is that current procedures for the construction of achievement tests do not provide an unambiguous basis for generalization to a well defined universe of content. At worst, achievement tests consist of arbitrary collections of items thrown together in a haphazard manner. At best, such tests consist of items judged by subject matter experts to be relevant to and representative of some incompletely defined universe of content. In neither case can it be said that there is an unambiguous basis for generalization. This is because the method of generating items and the criteria for the inclusion of items in the test cannot be stated in operational terms.
>
> The time-honored way out of this dilemma has been to resort to statistical and mathematical strategies in an attempt to generalize beyond the arbitrary collection of items in the test. By far the most popular of these strategies has been to invoke the concept of a latent variable—an underlying continuum which represents a hypothetical dimension of knowledge or skill [Osburn, 1968: 95].

It is clear from Osburn's argument that the existence of a universe of items is very important to the R-S approach. The difficulties inherent in such concepts were discussed by Loevinger (1965), although in view of the algorithms reviewed in the preceding section she may have overstated the case. She noted that the term population (universe) implies that in principle one can catalog, or display, or index all possible members even though the population (universe) is infinite and the catalogue cannot be completed. . . . No system is conceivable by which an index of all possible tests (items) could be drawn up. *There is no generating principle* [Loevinger, 1965: 147; italics added].

In Osburn's description, the L-T model is seen as a last resort, useful only when the item pool has not been carefully developed. However, there is nothing in the L-T model that prevents it from being applied to a situation in which there is an item universe. Indeed, Shoemaker and Osburn (1970), like Cronbach and Azuma (1962) before them, have found the assumption of a latent trait model useful in the investigation of the R-S model. Briefly, since the implications of the R-S model can sometimes become intractable, researchers have found it expedient to simulate data according to the assumptions of an L-T model— specifically, the two-parameters normal ogive model (which will be discussed later). Thus, in principle there is nothing incompatible between the R-S and L-T approaches. One may then wonder why must there be two psychometric models. To answer that question we must discuss what each model has to offer and how one goes about applying the model in practice.

Random Sampling Model

The mathematical underpinnings of the R-S model have been explicated by Cronbach et al. (1972) and Lord and Novick (1968: chap. 11). The foremost assumption in the theory is that there is a universe of items from which random samples can be drawn. The universe can be differentiated into facets, but for the present purposes I shall concentrate on universes with a single facet. The theory is mainly concerned with two problems. One is the problem of estimating the universe score, the second assessing how generalizable that estimate is. Of the two problems, the second occupies most of the theory by far. Unlike the classical model, in generalizability theory the error depends on the particular application. The classical model, by contrast, avoids much of the problem by insisting on the availability of parallel tests and ignoring incidental sources of error. The task of estimating generalizability coefficients is done by means of the methodology of analysis of variance. This methodology began to infiltrate psychometrics in the 1940s, as seen in the work of Burt (1955), Hoyt (1941), and Lindquist (1953). The work of Lindquist paved the way for generalizability theory, which was later developed by Cronbach and his associates (1963; Cronbach et al., 1972).

ESTIMATING UNIVERSE SCORES

A universe score refers to the score a testee would obtain if the entire universe of items was the test. Since in principle the universe of items is infinitely large, in principle the universe score cannot be observed. This means that it must be estimated, and (as do all estimates) it contains a certain amount of error.

Proportion correct. Perhaps the most intuitive way to summarize performance on a set of items is to compute the proportion of items answered correctly. If those items have been drawn at random from the universe, then this proportion is an unbiased estimate of the proportion of items in the universe that person can answer correctly (see Lord and Novick, 1968: chap. 11). This is so even when the items in the universe may be heterogeneous with respect to content, just as long as the sampling of items from the universe is random. The meaningfulness of a score derived in this fashion depends on content validity, not on response homogeneity. More concretely, to the extent that one agrees with the content of the universe, the proportion correct score is a meaningful and statistically unbiased summary of a testee's responses without any further transformation (Harris et al., 1977).

It should be noted that these properties of the proportion-correct score are maintained even when different testees are administered different items. The possibility that different persons respond to different items—as opposed to the usual situation, in which everyone responds to the same set of items—leads to the distinction between the *nested* and *crossed* testing designs. A one-facet nested design applies to the situation in which each testee responds to a set of items randomly sampled from the universe for him or her. The crossed design applies to the situation in which a random sample of items has been drawn from the universe, but the same set is administered to each student. The crossed design is the typical testing situation.

Regressed estimates. The appeal and simplicity of proportion correct is achieved by sacrificing information that could be used to improve the estimate. Regressed estimates are computationally more complex but are also more precise. Moreover, they have a conceptual appeal of their own because they incorporate collateral and prior information into the estimate. The incorporation of collateral information may be seen in the regression formulas for estimating the universe score in the nested and crossed cases.

For the nested case the formula is

$$\hat{\mu}_p = \rho^2 X_{pI} - \rho^2 \mu + \mu = \rho^2(X_{pI} - \mu) + \mu \qquad [1]$$

The formula for the crossed case is

$$\mu_p = \xi\rho^2 X_{pI} - \xi\rho^2 \mu_I + \mu = \xi\rho^2(X_{pI} - \mu_I) + \mu \qquad [2]$$

where

μ_p = estimated universe score for the pth person;

X_{pI} = observed test score for the pth person on a given set of I items;

$\rho^2, \xi\rho^2$ = generalizability coefficients under the nested and crossed cases, respectively;

μ = grand mean test score over the population of testees and universe of items;

μ_I = mean test score over the population of testees on a given set of I items.

The structure of the estimate is the same in both cases. Each is a linear combination of observed performance, X_{pI}, and the performance of the group to which the testee belongs. In the crossed case, since everyone responds to the same set of items, the measure of group performance is μ_I. In the nested case, since everyone takes a different set of items, μ is the measure of group performance.

Equations 1 and 2 are identical in form to Kelley's (1947) estimate of true score in the classical model. As pointed out by Novick and Jackson (1974), Kelley's formula represents a form of Bayesian estimate. Viewed as a Bayesian estimate, the psychometric assumptions behind the Kelley formula are that the observed scores for each individual are normally distributed, with a mean equal to that person's true (universe) score and a standard deviation that is the same for all individuals. The true or universe scores are also assumed to be normally distibuted. Clearly, the justifications of equation 1 or 2 as an estimate of the universe score requires more assumptions within a Bayesian framework than within the generalizability approach. Within the generalizability approach no distributional assumptions are made, but it is assumed that persons and items are sampled at random. Within a Bayesian approach no sampling assumptions are made, but distributional assumptions are required.

It should be stated that the proportion-correct and regressed estimates of individuals within a single group have a rank correlation of 1, and so it may be argued that they are interchangeable. However, if the scores are being used to select individuals above a certain score, different individuals would "pass" under the two methods of estimation. Furthermore, if individuals from different groups are being considered, then two individuals with the same observed score may not necessarily pass under the regressed-estimate approach. Instead, if both individuals are above their respective group means, then the one from the group with the higher mean will obtain a higher estimated universe score (Novick and Jackson, 1974; Cronbach et al., 1972).

More refined Bayesian estimates. Within a Bayesian approach the Kelley formula is, in a sense, a primitive estimator that needed a Bayesian structure to completely justify its applicability. This Bayesian structure has been developed by Lindley and Smith (1972) and rigorously applied by Novick and colleagues (e.g., Novick and Jackson, 1974; Lewis et al., 1975). The developments relevant to the problem of estimating domain scores from a Bayesian perspective have been surveyed by Hambleton, Swaminathan, Algina, and Coulson (1978) and need not be reviewed here. It should be pointed out, however, that these developments are not based on the assumption of random sampling from a universe. Instead, the assumption of exchangeability is often used in its place (although additional distributional assumptions are still required). Briefly, exchangeability (see e.g., Lindley and Phillips, 1976) is a property of a sequence of events—for instance, binary responses to a set of items. Such a sequence has the property of exchangeability if the probability of any sequence of responses containing the same number of 1s and 0s is the same. Exchangeability is a subjective notion, and therein lies a potential problem: What to me may appear exhangeable may not appear so to you. One way of avoiding this difficulty is by reintroducing random sampling (see Wang et al., 1977). That is, as long as items are sampled at random, it is more reasonable to argue that response vectors with the same number of "rights" and "wrongs" are exchangeable.

Bayesian methodology has often been applied in the context of criterion-referenced or domain-referenced tests. Such tests are distinguished from other tests in that performance is compared to an absolute standard rather than to the performance of others, as in norm-referenced tests. Implicit in this distinction is that criterion-referenced tests are measures of achievement that are informative in their own right. However, regressed estimates—including Bayesian estimates—because they utilize collateral and prior information in the form of distributional parameters of the population to which the individual is thought to belong, are far from normless. While the obtained estimate is not related to the distributions of scores, as in norm-referenced tests, the distribution of scores actually determines to some extent the magnitude of the score. This should be inadmissible to advocates of a criterion-referenced point of view. In criterion-referenced measurement, the estimate of what the individual can do should depend only on his or her performance on the test and not on the performance of the population to which an individual belongs.

When several groups are under consideration, the use of regressed and Bayesian estimates can be especially troublesome in a criterion-referenced context. For instance, it is common in many instructional settings to group students by abilities without necessarily segregating them into different classrooms. To avoid using this information in estimating domain scores would be contradictory to the entire rationale behind the Bayesian approach. On the other hand, to use the information would be contradictory to the rationale behind criterion-referenced measurement, where each point along the scale of performance is supposed to have a concrete meaning as to what the individual can do. Although it is possible to differentiate between the situation in which one is dealing with an entire group and in which one is dealing with an individual (see Lewis et al., 1975), the universe score still depends on observed performance, group performance, and prior beliefs or information.

ASSESSING THE GENERALIZABILITY OF SCORES

The richness of generalizability theory is apparent in its multitude of generalizability coefficients. Unlike the classical model, which admits only one generalizability coefficient—namely, reliability—within generalizability theory scores derived from a testing procedure can have a number of generalizability coefficients, depending on which factors affecting the measurement process have been taken into consideration. In each case the definition of generalizability is the same, namely the ration of universe score variance to observed score variance. If the different variance components corresponding to different conditions of administration have been previously estimated, it is possible to estimate the generalizability of scores under a given subset of conditions by making use of the variance component estimates.

For these purposes, however, I shall consider only with "one-facet" designs, that is, the situations in which a number of testees take a test. No other information—for example, conditions of administration—is taken into consideration. Within this limited scope, however, the distinction between the crossed and nested designs is still apparent. For both the nested and crossed cases generalizability is estimated by (see Brennan, 1983)

$$\hat{\xi\rho}^2 = \frac{\hat{\sigma}^2(p)}{\sigma^2(p) + \hat{\sigma}^2(\delta)} \tag{3}$$

where

$\hat{\sigma}^2(p)$ = estimate of the variance associated with persons or testees;
$\hat{\sigma}^2(\delta)$ = error variance.

To estimate this coefficient, we conduct a two-way analysis of variance (ANOVA), in which items are the levels of one factor and persons are the level of the second factor. The purpose of this analysis is to obtain the expected mean squares associated with $\sigma^2(p)$ and $\sigma^2(\delta)$, which are given by

	Nested Case	Crossed Case
$\hat{\sigma}^2(p)$	$\dfrac{MS(p) - (1 - n_i/N_i)MS(i{:}p)}{n_i}$	$\dfrac{MS(p) - (1 - n_i/N_i)MS(ip)}{n_i}$
$\hat{\sigma}^2(\delta)$	$\dfrac{(1 - n_i/N_i)MS(i{:}p)}{n_i}$	$\dfrac{(1 - n_i/N_i)MS(ip)}{n_i}$

where

$MS(p)$ = is the mean squares for persons;
n_i = number of items in the study;
N_i = number of items in the universe;

MS(i:p) = mean squares for interaction of persons and items for the nested case;

MS(ip) = mean square for interaction of persons and items for the crossed case.

Substituting the appropriate terms in equation 3, we obtain for the crossed case

$$\hat{\xi\rho}^2 = \frac{MS(p) - (1 - n_i/N_i)MS(ip)}{MS(p)} \qquad [4a]$$

which is equivalent to the usual KR-20 reliability coefficient when items are fixed rather than sampled from a universe. For the nested case we have

$$\hat{\xi\rho}^2 = \frac{MS(p) - (1 - n_i/N_i)MS(i:p)}{MS(p)} \qquad [4b]$$

Generalizability coefficients are one form of expressing how well the observed score estimates the universe score. Brennan and Kane (1977) have derived from generalizability theory a different type of coefficient, which they call signal-to-noise ratios. Their work is illuminating in that, within the same framework, they derive such measures for universe scores, norm-referenced scores, and mastery tests in a one-facet crossed design. We shall discuss only the first two in what follows.

The item-observed score is modeled by

$$X_{pi} = \mu + \pi_p + \beta_i + \pi\beta_i + e \qquad [5]$$

where

μ = grand mean in the population of persons and the universe of items;

πp = effect for person p;

β_i = effect for item i;

$\pi\beta_i$ = effect of the interaction for person p and item i;

e = random error.

It is assumed that each effect is sampled independently and that the expected value for each effect is zero.

The key to the Brennan-Kane formulation lies in the two definitions of error of measurement possible within the generalizability framework. If the scores are used to estimate universe scores, then error of measurement, or noise, for the pth testee is defined as

$$\Delta_p = X_{pI} - \mu_p \qquad [6]$$

that is, the difference between the person's observed score and his universe score. The variance of Δ_p denoted by $\sigma^2(\Delta_p)$ is called the power of the noise. On the other hand, if the person's absolute score is not of interest, but its relative standing within his population is, then the error of measurement is

$$\delta_p = (X_{pI} - \mu_I) - (\mu_p - \mu) \qquad [7]$$

The first term is the pth person's observed deviation score; the second term is the "true" deviation score; their difference is the error of measurement when deviation rather than absolute scores are of interest. The variance of δ_p denoted by $\sigma^2(\delta_p)$ is the power of the noise for this case.

In both cases the signal is defined as

$$\text{signal} = \mu_p - \mu \qquad [8]$$

and then its variance is the power of the signal, that is,

$$S = \epsilon_p (\mu_p - \mu)^2 \qquad [9]$$

where ϵ_p denotes expectation over persons. For the estimations of these components see Brennan and Kane (1977). The signal-to-noise ratio is simply

$$\lambda_1 = S/\sigma^2(\Delta_p) \qquad [10]$$

when absolute or domain scores are of interest; and

$$\lambda_2 = S/\sigma^2(\delta_p) \qquad [11]$$

when deviation scores are of interest.

As indicated earlier, the Brennan-Kane formulation assumes a crossed design, in which everyone takes the same items. It is interesting to note, (although Brennan and Kane did not mention it) that under a nested design, since $\sigma^2(\Delta_p) = \sigma^2(\delta_p)$, both signal-noise ratios are identical. This seems to blur somewhat the distinction between criterion- (i.e., absolute) and norm-referenced test scores.

ITEM ANALYSIS

The R-S model is oriented to the test score level rather than the item level. This seems to be a function of the reliance on the existence of a universe of items in which all items are good. As a result, within the R-S model there is not a formal way of describing the characteristics of the items that compose a test. Domain- or criterion-referenced tests that depend on the R-S model for their mathematical underpinnings are thus devoid of a formal procedure of assessing item characteristics. As a result, sometimes test developers blindly use item statistics that were originally developed for norm-referenced tests, with criterion-referenced tests. The difficulties to which this leads is illustrated in discussion of test score variance.

It is implicit in many writers' minds (e.g., Popham and Husek, 1969) that variability in achievement testing has no legitimate role; thus item indices, which also utilize observed score variance, have no legitimate role. The argument, however, seems to rest on pedagogical rather than psychometric considerations. Certainly the distinction between absolute and normative scores can be easily accommodated within the R-S model, as Brennan and Kane (1977) demonstrated, without resorting to any assumptions about the magnitude of the variability of test scores. There are, in fact, indications that proponents of criterion-referenced measurement are beginning to accept variability as a legitimate concept. For example, Hambleton et al. (1978: 36) noted that

> While variability is not a factor in test construction, neither is it a completely useless concept. Indeed, variability will be observed when a sample is heterogeneous in terms of their domain scores. By establishing a priori the composition of an examinee sample, the resulting variability will provide additional helpful information for assessing test items.

They approved classical methods of assessing item quality but emphasized that such indices should be used to detect items in need of revision, rather than to select items for inclusion in a test.

APPLICATION TO
THE ASSESSMENT OF GROUPS

Achievement testing often has the dual purpose of measuring the individual on the one hand, and to serve as a means of evaluating instruction on the other. The R-S model can be easily molded to serve the latter function. Consider the not uncommon task of evaluating the effectiveness of a large-scale intervention program with respect to achievement, or the task of monitoring achievement levels at an aggregate level, as in state assessment programs. Typically, in such situations there are thousands of participants. The information needed is not how each and every student performs but the distribution of those scores; more often than not, the mean and standard deviation of the distribution are all that is needed.

The design that first comes to mind for collecting such information is to administer the same test to every recipient of the program or member of the aggregate. As it turns out, this is a statistically inefficient way of doing it. If a universe of items is available, a far more efficient procedure is to select a random sample of recipients of size N and to administer to each a distinct random sample of items. This design is the one-facet nested design discussed earlier in connection with generalizability and signal-to-noise coefficients.

The sampling variance of the mean test score for the nested design is estimated without bias (see Lord, 1977a) by

$$\text{VAR}(\bar{X}) = [N^2(n-1)]^{-1} \sum_{p=1}^{N} X_p(n - X^p) \qquad [12]$$

where

N = number of testees;
n = number of items administered;
X_p = p^{th} person number-right score.

For the crossed case, however,

$$\text{VAR}(\bar{X}) = (n - 1)^{-1} (n^2 s_d^2) \qquad [13]$$

where

$$s_d^2 = \sum_{i=1}^{n} (d_i^2 / n) - \bar{d}^2 \qquad [14]$$

d_i = difficulty of the ith item;
$\bar{d}$ = mean difficulty.

It is assumed that testees are fixed and that the universe of items is infinite.

The important feature to note is that, for the nested case, the number of testees used to estimate the mean enters into the determination of the variance of the mean, whereas this is not the case for the crossed case. Thus, whenever there are large numbers of potential testees and a large pool of items from which to draw a set of items for each individual, the nested design is to be preferred for estimating mean group achievement.

Although in many large-scale evaluations of instructional programs there are plenty of testees, often there is not a large pool of items from which to assemble a test for each testee. Even if there were, the logistic problem of assembling and administering individual tests in the field would be monumental and possibly infeasible without the help of computer administration. Under those circumstances the technology of matrix sampling (Lord and Novick, 1968: chap. 11; Sirotnick, 1974; Wellington, 1976) is applicable. In matrix sampling random samples of testees are formed into a subgroup. Then tests are drawn at random without replacement from the universe of items. (The nested design just discussed can be seen as the limiting case of this situation when subgroups of 1 are formed). In many applications, however, there is no "universe of items" but, rather, a long test (or pool) of items. The procedure then calls for dividing the long test into nonoverlapping subtests. Procedures for the situation in which items are drawn with replacement have also been discussed (see, e.g., Sirotnick, 1974).

Latent Trait Model

The specialization of the R-S model into the so-called classical model, as described by Gulliksen (1950), has been the psychometric backbone of achievement testing over the last several decades. During the 1940s a new measurement theory began to form with the work of Ferguson (1942), Lawley (1943), and Tucker (1946); later came Lord (1952), Lazarsfeld (1959), and Rasch (1960). Today the theory is known as latent trait theory, "item characteristic curve" (ICC) theory, or more recently (Lord, 1980a), "item response theory (IRT). The results of this new theory up to 1968 are to be found in the treatises by Lord and Novick (1968) and Birnbaum (1968). Since then the theory has expanded in a number of ways, as seen in the work of Bock (1972) and Samejima (1969, 1972, 1973, 1974), as well as many European psychometricians (e.g., see Fischer and Formann, 1982). There are indications that the theory is now reaching the practitioner and may in fact prove to be the "standard" psychometric model.

The L-T and R-S models differ considerably in their details; however, the key distinction is that L-T does not resort to random sampling from a universe or the existence of parallel forms to justify its results. Instead, it is postulated that performance of a given item is a function of the testee's position on a continuum or a trait, and of random error. The price of forsaking random sampling is the estimation of that function, a process known as "item parameter estimation" or "item calibration."

Just as random sampling is difficult to implement, the biggest practical obstacle in implementing the L-T approach is to estimate the relationship between the probability of answering the item correctly and achievement. That relationship is described by the item characteristic curve. To estimate it, the assumption of local independence (Lazarsfeld, 1959; Lord and Novick, 1968: chap. 16) is necessary. This assumption implies that performance on a set of items depends only on the person's position on the trait and random error. That is, the following linear model holds:

$$\gamma_g = \rho_g \theta + \epsilon_g \qquad [15]$$

where

γ_g	=	latent response to item g;
θ	=	the trait (in this case, achievement);
ρ_g	=	regression coefficient of γ on θ;
ϵ_g	=	random error component.

such that the ϵs are uncorrelated with each other and θ. The assumption stated in this form is reminiscent of one assumption in the R-S model, namely that the "effects" are sampled independently and are therefore uncorrelated.

It is clear that local independence implies unidimensionality (and vice versa) in the present context. It is important to emphasize that in the absence of other information, this unidimensional trait is a statistical fabrication to account for the covariation among responses to a set of items. Now, if the items have been chosen in such a way that they are related to educational objectives, there is some justification for calling θ "achievement," although ultimately validation studies are required to determine if that interpretation is justified. That θ is unobservable and on a metric to which most are unaccustomed is not a real distinction with the R-S model, since the universe score is also unobservable.

It should be pointed out that unidimensionality does not imply that performance on the items is due to single psychological process. In fact, a variety of psychological processes are involved in the act of responding to a set of items. However, as long as they function in unison—that is, the performance on each item is affected by the same processes and in the same form—unidimensionality will hold. As a violation of this principle, consider an achievement test, some of the items in which call for numerical computation, whereas the rest of the items call for the recall of factual material. If within the populations being tested with this instrument there is variability with respect to numerical ability, then performance on the test as a whole will depend on that ability and achievement.

What follows is a brief survey of the variety of models within the theory. We shall then concentrate on one aspect of the theory, namely dichotomous models, to discuss the problem of estimating ICCs, assessing the fit of the model, estimating θ, and assessing the error of measurement in θ. For other introductions to L-T or IRT models the reader is referred to Hambleton and Cook (1977), Hambleton (1979), and Bejar (1983). For reviews, the reader should consult Hambleton, Swaminathan, Cook, Eignor, and Gifford (1978) and Traub and Wolfe (1981).

SURVEY OF
LATENT TRAIT MODELS

One distinctive feature of latent trait theory is the variety of models it has produced. This feature can, however, prove to be a source of confusion initially. Therefore, we shall outline in this section a scheme for the classification of latent trait models to guide readers who may wish to pursue this literature, but here the emphasis will be on models for items that are scored with two categories. The scheme consists of three classification variables: response levels, parametric structures, and statistical assumptions. A fourth classification variable is possible, namely the dimensionality of the latent space. That is, in principle, there is a multivariate counterpart to each of the univariate models.

Response level. This is the most basic way of classifying models, because it is intimately linked with the kind of data to be analyzed. Three levels can be distinguished: dichotomous, polychotomous, and continuous. In the *dichotomous response level,* responses to an item are reduced to one of two categories. In the case of ability and achievement testing, these two categories are "right" and "wrong"; in personality measurement they may be "agree" and "disagree." The important point is that even if the possible responses are, say, five, they are reduced to two categories.

The next response level may be referred to as the *polychotomous response level.* As the name implies, here responses to an item are not reduced to two categories. There might still be a reduction from a large number of possible answers, but as long as the response categories are three or more, the polychotomous response level applies.

Finally, there is the *continuous response level,* which may be thought of as the limiting case of the polychotomous situation; that is, the case in which the number of response categories in infinitely large. Usually this response mode calls for item formats very different from those used in the dichotomous and polychotomous models. For example, the continuous response may be useful when the response is latency, or the reported subjective probability that some statement is true (see Bejar, 1977).

Parametric structure. The parametric structure has to do with the assumptions that are made about the psychological process behind the responses to the items in the test. In the dichotomous level, three types of parametric structure have been described, namely the one-, two-, and three-parameter models. The one-parameter case pertains if the items in the test differ only in difficulty. In that case each item is described by a single parameter, namely, difficulty. If, in addition to difficulty, the items also differ with respect to their discriminating power, the two-parameter model holds. Finally, when the correct answer to an item may be found by guessing, a third parameter is required.

In the polychotomous case, two types of models are distinguished: the heterogeneous and the homogeneous (compare Samejima, 1972). The homogeneous case holds when the discriminating power of each of the response categories within a given item is the same. One may expect such a situation when there is a cumulative or stage process behind the response. The model predicts that the individual will most likely give a response consistent with his or her level of development. For example, the model has been applied with some success to responses to moral development questionnaires (Lieberman, 1973). The theory behind the questionnaire (Kohlberg, 1969) is that children go through a series of ordered stages of moral development, and so the graded model is justified a priori.

By contrast, in the heterogeneous case, it is not assumed that there is a stage process behind the response. Instead, it is assumed that an individual is attracted to a series of responses and that the response actually given is the one that exerts the most attraction for that individual. Unlike the homogeneous case, for the heterogeneous case it is not assumed that each response category has the same discriminating power. Application of polychotomous models can be found in Thissen (1976), Masters (1982), and Andrich (1978).

Since the continuous model is an extension of the polychotomous case, the distinction between the homogeneous nominal and heterogeneous graded model is also applicable, as Samejima (1973) has pointed out.

Statistical assumptions. The last classification variable for latent trait models has to do with the form of the error distribution or the variability left in the response after the individual's position in the latent trait has been taken care of, that is, ϵ in equation 15. If those residuals are distributed normally, the *normal-ogive* family of models obtains; if the distribution is assumed to be logistic, then the *logistic* family obtains. It is known that the normal and logistic distributions are very similar, and for some purposes it is not crucial which distribution is assumed. However, for other purposes—for example, scoring (Bejar and Weiss, 1979)—it can make a difference. Thus, it is best not to think of corresponding models from the two families as interchangeable.

Many of the results concerning the dichotomous response level are found in Lord and Novick (1968). Those about the polychotomous response level are in Samejima (1969, 1972) and Bock (1972). The results for the continuous response level are found in Samejima (1973). Multivariate extensions of the theory are discussed in Samejima (1974), Sympson (1977), and Whiteley (1980).

ICCs AND THEIR ESTIMATION

The key concept in the L-T model is the item characteristic curve (ICC). The term applies to the case in which responses are scored into two categories. Since it is not our purpose to review all the intricacies of the theory, our discussion will be limited for the most part to the dichotomous case.

Figure 1 shows ICC curves of the normal ogive variety for four items. Each curve has three distinctive characteristics. First, the ICCs differ with respect to their slopes at different points along θ; they also differ with respect to their inflection point, the point at which the slope changes from increasing to decreasing; finally, they differ with respect to their lower asymptote. Because items within a test will usually differ

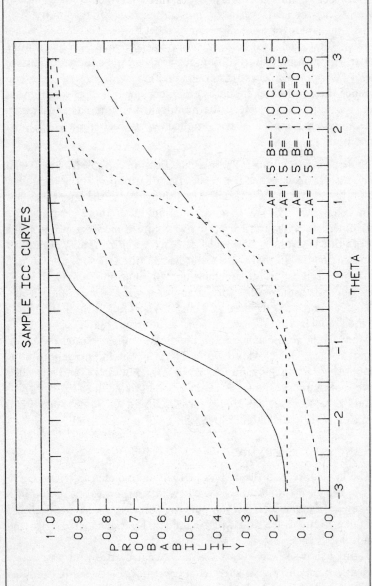

Figure 1 Plot of Four ICC Curves

with respect to all three characteristics, three parameters are necessary to fully describe the probability of success as a function of θ for each item. The parameter describing the slope of the ICC is denoted by a_g. More precisely, a_g is proportional to the slope of the ICC at the point of inflection. The point of inflection itself is referred to as the difficulty parameters, denoted by b_g. Finally, the lower asymptote, often referred to as the "guessing" parameters, is denoted by c_g. When we speak of estimating ICCs we are actually speaking of estimating a_g, b_g, and c_g.

If correct responses cannot be obtained by guessing, as in free-response items, the c_g is 0.0 for all items and may be ignored in the estimation of ICCs and later in the estimation of θ.

Also, when the a_g parameter does not differ across the items being considered, a_g need not be estimated. Models where only the difficulty is free to vary are referred to as one-parameter models. By far the most common of such models is the so-called Rasch model (Rasch, 1960; Wright, 1977).

The choice among a one-, two-, or three-parameter model would seem to depend on whether the items being considered differ with respect to each of those parameters. In reality the choice is not so simple. The three-parameter model was suggested by Birnbaum (1968) as a means of dealing with the possibility of answering an item correctly even if the testee is of very low ability. This typically occurs with multiple-choice items, and for that reason c_g is often referred to as the guessing parameter. A decision facing the user of a three-parameter model is whether to estimate c_g or to fix it to a constant—say, 1 divided by the number of alternatives. If one views c_g as an empirical property of the ICC affected by factors other than guessing, then the user will probably want to estimate c_g. Unfortunately, the estimation of c_g is difficult and imprecise, as shown in several simulation studies (e.g., Gugel et al., 1976), but improvements are occurring (see Messick et al., 1983: 43-48).

Advocates of one-parameter models, most notably Wright (1977), have taken the position that test construction should strive to avoid the occurrence of guessing—thus eliminating the need for a c_g parameter—and the presence of items with highly discrepant discriminations. It is easy to agree on the need to reduce the possibility of guessing, but it is not so clear why all items should be equally discriminating. Surely it is possible to find a subset of items within a pool with a common a_g, but most likely any large collection of items will be heterogeneous with respect to discrimination. Wright argues that in principle the a_g parameter is not estimable, and apparently, in his view it is best to assume it is a constant rather than attempt to estimate it for each item. This argument raises two questions: (1) Is a_g in fact unestimable? (2) What are the consequences of ignoring heterogeneity in a_g?

The first question can be answered by means of simulation studies in which test data are generated according to the model, and ICCs are estimated from the generated data. The true a_g is compared to the estimated a_g. Lord (1975) and Sympson (1978) have carried out such investigations and found that a_g can be estimated, although in comparison to the estimation of b_g, the estimation of a_g is subject to a considerable amount of error, even with large numbers of subjects and items. The consequences of ignoring a_g can be similarly investigated through simulation procedures, but little work seems to have been done in the area. However, Dinero and Haertel (1977) have shown that if the a_gs are rectangularly distributed, then θ is seriously misestimated.

Estimating ICCs. Although my aim in this review is to give a conceptual overview of the L-T model, it is appropriate to talk briefly about the estimation of ICCs, because the underlying principle is easily grasped and may further the understanding of the concept of an ICC. Suppose for the moment that we have on each of 1000 persons their true θ and their response to an item. Let us compute the proportion of correctly answering individuals within each of, say, twenty intervals from -3.00 to 3.00. If we were to plot the resulting proportions against the midpoint of the interval from which they came, we would find that the twenty points fall along the ICC. Having obtained the twenty points of the ICC, we can obtain the best-fitting ICC by a variety of curve-fitting procedures. Of course, in practice, we do not know the individual's true θ; therefore, to make this principle workable it is necessary to use estimates of θ.

The approach to estimating ICC just described is an instance of what Bock and Lieberman (1970) called the conditional approach to parameter estimation. It is conditional in the sense that θ must be estimated to carry out the estimation. They also described an unconditional approach that does not require the estimation of θ; instead, its distribution must be assumed. In general, successful estimation of item parameters by the conditional approach requires that testees respond to a large number of items. On the other hand, unconditional estimation can be carried out even when testees respond to as few as five items (see Bock and Lieberman, 1970). Readers interested in pursuing the extensive literature on item parameter estimation are referred to Lord (1980a), Bock and Aitkin (1981), Andersen (1982), Thissen (1982), and Swaminathan (1983).

ASSESSMENT OF MODEL FIT

Being able to estimate the ICCs is no guarantee that the model fits the data. In fact, the estimation programs will usually return reasonable-looking parameter estimates even when gross violations of the model are present (see Reckase, 1977). This suggests that the fit of the model should be examined by a variety of procedures. Thus, to investigate the reasonableness of the assumption of unidimensionality in a set of items, it is recommended that the interitem correlation matrix be factored and shown to have one largely predominant factor (Indow and Samejima, 1966). Another approach especially useful in achievement testing has been described by Bejar (1980a) and appears to be more powerful than factor analysis of interitem correlations matrices in detecting subtle deviations from the model.

The fit of a latent trait model is defined with respect to all the populations that will be tested by the testing instrument. Thus, a more stringent and appropriate test of fit requires that, within each population, the unidimensionality assumption holds, and, in addition, the parameter estimates in one population have a linear relationship with the parameter estimates in another population. That is, it must be shown that the item parameters are invariant across populations of testees (see Lord and Novick, 1968; chap. 16).

The notion of invariance has been the subject of some confusion in the applications of the L-T model. Wood (1976: 252) called it one of the grayest areas of test theory. In some discussions of invariance it has been implied that the model guarantees invariant item parameters in the sense that if one estimates item parameters for any set of data, the resulting estimates will have the invariance property. In reality, invariance holds only if the model fits. Since fit is defined with respect to all populations envisioned as taking the test, and parameter stimulation is seldom carried out simultaneously across populations (but see Bejar, 1977), it seems best to view invariance as a measure of fit of the model across populations of testees. Thus, a rigorous test of fit of an L-T model would consist of showing each parameter linearly related across populations. As Wood (1976) noted, however, evidence of invariance is conspicuous by its absence. However, in one investigation (Bejar et al., 1977) it was shown that the difficulty and, to some extent, the discrimination parameters were invariant across samples of testees taking the same course during different quarters.

What evidence is there that latent-trait models fit actual test data in general and achievement test data in particular? There is a considerable amount of evidence that latent-trait models do fit actual test data. Not surprisingly, attempts to answer this question are most abundant in the context of the Rasch model, since so much research has been done on it. According to Rentz and Rentz (1979), the model has been successfully applied by many investigators and to many content areas. Whiteley and Dawis (1976), however, found that when using an external criterion of fit—namely, whether the context in which the items appeared affected difficulty, the Rasch model did not fit well.

There is also a growing body of evidence that the three-parameter model fits both aptitude test data (e.g., Bejar and Wingersky, 1982) and achievement test data (e.g., Bejar et al., 1977). A question of more practical importance is whether some models fit better than others. Implicit in this last question is the conception that model selection should be guided by which model fits the data better. In a rare investigation Hambleton and Traub (1973) actually compared the fit of the one- and two-parameter models to the same data (SAT item responses). They found that the two-parameter model was an improvement under some conditions. In practice, however, adoption of model is based on practical considerations. For example, the choice between normal ogive and logistic models is often based on pragmatic considerations, i.e., whether the available item calibration program uses one or the other model. To some extent this may be justified on the grounds that test-of-fit criteria are not sufficiently powerful to discriminate between both types of models. Lord (1980a), however, has suggested that since the logistic model is less affected by careless mistakes, it may be preferable to the normal ogive.

The choice of the number of parameters is also often guided by arbitrary decision rules. Some researchers would not consider anything but a one-parameter model because of the difficulties in estimation in two- and three-parameter models, even though a better fit could be obtained by taking into account heterogeneity in discrimination and nonzero lower asymptotes. Lord (forthcoming) has shown that when the sample size available for parameter estimation is small, these researchers would be doing the right thing. In general, however, a more detailed analysis would be necessary to arrive at a conclusion. Waller (1980) has described a useful approach.

Ultimately, it would seem that the criterion of fit should be whether the fit is good enough for the intended application. Slinde and Linn (1978) evaluated the one-parameter logistic model in a vertical equating application and concluded that it was not entirely appropriate. Unfortunately, they did not investigate whether a two- or three-parameter model would serve any better, nor was it clear that the problem was due to ignoring variability in discrimination and nonzero lower asymptote. In any event, the test to which they put the model was very severe, since it involved groups of widely differing abilities. In a subsequent investigation Slinde and Linn (1979) found that, despite substantial lack of fit, the mean and standard deviation of different tests were successfully equated. However, Marco et al. (1980) found that often the three-parameter model gives better equating results than the one-parameter model; even when the one-parameter gives adequate results the three-parameter is likely to give still better results.

Similarly, Reckase (1977) compared the one- and three-parameter logistics on a number of criteria and showed that, if the objective of measurement is to rank individuals, then both models give equally good results.

More work is obviously needed to evaluate the consequences of employing any one model for a specific application. The methodology for accomplishing this is evolving gradually (e.g., Hambleton and Murray, 1983; van den Wollenberg, 1982). As that information accumulates, we will be in a better position to choose one model over the other for any particular application. For an incisive review of the issues, see Traub (1983).

ESTIMATION OF θ AND PRECISION OF MEASUREMENT

The estimation of ICCs and assessment of fit are procedures that require large resources and expertise. The nature of the problem is such that it is not likely that parameter estimation will be done locally. It is more likely that calibrated pools of items may be made available to schools. Once the parameters are in hand, it is possible to focus on the problem of estimating achievement and the precision of the estimates. Those topics are discussed in this section.

After the ICCs have been estimated, the process of estimating θ is a conceptually straightforward procedure. Numerically, however, the estimation of θ usually requires computer programs, which fortunately need not be very difficult to develop (see Bejar and Weiss, 1980). There are three types of estimation procedures currently being used. We shall discuss each of them and comment on their interrelationship. We shall also comment on differences among the logistic and normal ogive models and relate these differences to their implicit conceptualization of achievement.

Maximum likelihood estimates. Within the L-T model the probability of answering an item correctly is conditional on θ and the item parameters and is described by the ICC. We can likewise speak of the probability of a response vector. A response vector is simply the pattern of 1s and 0s given in response to a set of items. In a two-item test there are four possible response vectors, namely $(1,1)$, $(0,1)$, $(1,0)$, and $(0,0)$. In general, in an n-item test there are 2^n response vectors. The probability of a response vector for a given θ is the product of the probabilities across items and is denoted by

$$P_v(\theta) = \Pi P_g(\theta)^{u_g} [1 - P_g(\theta)]^{(1-u_g)} \qquad [16]$$

where

$P_v(\theta)$ = probability of response vector v;

$P_g(\theta)$ = probability of answering the item correctly conditional on θ and the item parameters, i.e., the ICC;

u_g = 1 if the item is answered correctly,
0 if the item is answered incorrectly.

We are allowed to take the product of probabilities by virtue of the local independence assumption discussed earlier.

Equation 16 is also the likelihood function of response vector v. A likelihood function simply gives the likelihood of a fixed response vector as a function of values of θ. The value of θ for which the likelihood is a maximum is the maximum likelihood estimate of θ and is denoted by $\hat{\theta}$.

Unfortunately, for most models there is not an explicit formula for $\hat{\theta}$. However, if all the items under consideration are equivalent—that is, have the same ICC—then there is an explicit formula. For the normal ogive case it is

$$\hat{\theta} = \frac{b + \phi^{-1}(\bar{u})}{a} \qquad [17]$$

where b and a are the difficulty and discrimination parameters common to all items,

ϕ^{-1} + inverse of the normal cumulative function;

u + proportion of items answered correctly.

For the logistic model the formula is

$$\hat{\theta} = \frac{b + \log[\bar{u}/(1 - \bar{u})]}{Da} \qquad [18]$$

where $(D = 1.7)$ is a scaling factor to put the estimate on the same metric as the normal ogive.

For the one- and two-parameter logistic models, although there is not an explicit formula for θ, there is a sufficient statistic associated with the model (see Birnbaum, 1968: chap. 18; Andersen, 1977). For the two-parameter model that statistic is

$$t = \Sigma u_g a_g \qquad [19]$$

that is, the sum of the item discrimination of the items answered correctly. For the one-parameter logistic model the statistic is

$$t = (\Sigma u_g)/n \qquad [20]$$

or the proportion of items answered correctly. A practical implication of the existence of a sufficient statistic is that there is a one-to-one correspondence between t and θ, which may considerably simplify the estimation of θ. Thus, in the one-parameter model there are only n possible θs to consider. For the one-, two-, and three-parameter normal ogive models and for the three-parameter logistic there are no sufficient statistics, but there is a unique and different θ associated with every possible response vector except two, namely, answering all items correctly or incorrectly.

Bayesian mean and modal estimates. In maximum likelihood estimation no specific assumption is made with regard to the distribution of θ. However, it is often the case that the population to which any individual belongs is known. If the tester is willing to make an assumption about the shape and parameters of the distribution, Bayesian procedures can be used to incorporate that information. Samejima (1969: chap. 7), Owen (1975), and Swaminathan (1983) have discussed such procedures. Owen (1975) has discussed a procedure that assumes that θ is normally distributed. The mean and variance of the distribution after the last item is scored are taken to be the estimated θ and its error, respectively. Samejima (1969) has also discussed a procedure that, instead of taking the means of the posterior distribution as the estimate, takes the mode as the distribution, which she called Bayes modal estimate.

Viewed from a Bayesian perspective, the relationship between maximum likelihood estimators and Bayesian estimators is that, in the former, it is implicitly assumed that the "prior" distribution of θ is rectangular. Sympson (1977) had discussed these and other relationships among Bayesian and maximum likelihood estimators of θ.

Conceptualization of achievement implicit in different scoring procedures. In applications of the L-T model in which the concern is not with the individual scores, the scoring procedure used is probably not very important. For instance, if we are correlating scores from several tests, the correlations are not likely to change appreciably when different scoring procedures are used. On the other hand, in achievement and selection testing, the concern is with the individual, and the scoring procedure could affect decisions about an individual.

The different "scoring philosophies" of the normal ogive and logistic models were first pointed out by Samejima (1969). In general, the logistic model is "discrimination oriented," whereas the normal ogive is "difficulty oriented." In determining a score, the logistic model rewards testees who answer discriminating items correctly. This can be seen in the sufficient statistic associated with a response vector. That sufficient statistic is just the sum of the item discrimination of the items answered correctly for the two-parameter case; for the one-parameter (Rasch) model, in which discrimination is constant, it is the proportion of items answered correctly. Thus, with the Rasch model, testees answering correctly an equal proportion of items would be estimated to have the same achievement level, regardless of the difficulties of the items. For example, testee A may answer correctly the 40% most difficult items in the test, and testee B may answer correctly the 40% easiest items. Both testees will be estimated to have the same θ level. If this appears counter-intuitive, proponents of the model remind us that testee A also missed the 60% easiest items, and testee B missed only 40%. Nevertheless, lay persons seem to object to this scoring philosophy (see Owen, 1983: 31).

In contrast to the logistic model, the normal ogive model is difficulty oriented. This means that students are rewarded by answering correctly the most difficult items. Thus, in the above example, testee A would be estimated to have a higher achievement level than testee B.

To illustrate these differences, consider a five-item test with discrimination given by $a_1 = a_3 = a_5 = 1.0$ and $a_2 = a_4 = 1.50$; $b_1 = -2.00$, $b_2 = -1.00$, $b_3 = 0.0$, $b_4 = 1.00$, $b_5 = 2.00$. Table 1 shows the maximum likelihood

TABLE 1
Comparison of the Scoring Procedures

	Response Pattern	Maximum Likelihood	
		Normal	Logistic
1	00001	−.93	−1.60
2	10000	−1.63	−1.60
3	00011	−.13	−.46
4	11000	−.42	−.46
5	00111	.13	.46
6	11100	.42	.46

estimates of θ under the logistic and normal ogive models for several response vectors.

The potential differences between scoring procedures is best seen in the first response pattern. According to the normal ogive, $\hat{\theta} = -.93$ and $\theta = -1.60$, according to the logistic model. That is, a testee would get a higher score in the normal ogive model by virtue of answering correctly a very difficult item.

The above paragraphs show some of the implications of different scoring procedures for achievement testing purposes. The examples were deliberately chosen to illustrate the potential differences. In practice, the differences may be less evident because tests are normally longer than five items, and, as the number of items increase, differences are also likely to disappear. Moreover, the probability of "odd" response patterns in which only the difficult items are answered correctly becomes lower as the number of items increases. Nevertheless, the differing conceptualizations of achievement implicit in the normal and logistic models can serve, as Samejima (1969) suggested, to choose one of them for practical applications.

Assessment of precision of measurement. Once we have estimated θ, we need to worry about the precision of that estimate. One of the most important concepts to emerge from the L-T model is the notion of information. Unlike reliability and generalizability, information is a *local* measure of precision of measurement. That is, precision of measurement is assessed at each level of θ; hence we speak of information functions. Also, unlike reliability and generalizability, information is a property of the testing procedure, whereas generalizability is a property of the scores derived under a given testing procedure, set of circumstances, and sample of individuals. In this sense, information is a more general and, thus, more valuable index. The idea was anticipated by

Lord (1952), but it was not until Birnbaum (1968) and Samejima (1969) that the notion was formalized. Samejima (1969) described information as the expected value of the second derivative of the log-likelihood function. That is,

$$I(\theta) = E \left[\frac{\partial^2 L_v(\theta)}{\partial \theta} \right] \qquad [21]$$

Thus, psychometric information is identical to Fisher's information measure (see Edwards, 1972).

The justification of information as a measure of precision of measurement can be deduced from the properties of maximum likelihood estimators. As the number of items increases, the maximum likelihood estimate of θ can be shown (see Birnbaum, 1968: 457) to be normally distributed with mean θ and variance $1/I(\theta)$. Thus, information is seen to be the reciprocal of the variability of the maximum likelihood estimate of θ. It can also be shown (Kendall and Stuart, 1961: 8-10) that $1/I(\theta)$ is the minimum attainable variance in estimating θ. Thus, information is the best that can be done in terms of precision of measurement in estimating θ, at least asymptotically. Some empirical results by Samejima (1977), however, suggest that the asymptotic requirement can be satisfied with as few as twenty items. Clearly, further research is needed to establish the generality of her results. For instance, it is possible that the characteristics of the items involved may determine to some extent how many items are needed to achieve asymptotic conditions.

Apart from the asymptotic requirement, an equally important consideration in the validity of information as precision of measurement is the fit of the model to the data. This, of course, is true of any deduction from the model and may appear to be a platitude. Nevertheless, the following must be emphasized: Applying latent trait models involves a constant assessment of the fit of the model to the particular data to which it is applied. To illustrate, let test X consist of a series of verbally stated arithmetic problems, such that the verbal complexity of the problems varies across items. Suppose the test is calibrated on a population of testees, all of whom are of high verbal ability. In that population, responses will be a function solely of quantitative ability and the ICCs will reflect the relationship of performance on the items and the continuum of quantitative ability. An individual drawn from that population will perform largely as a function of quantitative ability. The estimated θ and the associated information value will be accurate. Now consider an individual of low verbal ability. If he were to take the test, his performance on the entire test would be a function of both verbal and quantitative ability. Other things being equal, his performance on the verbally simple problems is likely to be better than performance on verbally complex problems. For this individual, the θ estimated from his response vector will not be an accurate estimate of his position on the trait of quantitative ability. For the same reason, the information value associated with the estimated θ will not be a realistic assessment of the precision of measurement for that individual.

In short, information as a measure of precision of measurement cannot be taken at face value since it is a deduction from the model. It is valid only to the extent that the process generating the responses for a given individual is the same as the process that generated the responses in the data used in the estimation of the item parameters.

Comparison of the Two Measurement Models

A major decision confronting the designer of an achievement testing system is the choice among measurement models. In this section we have outlined features of the two major models, namely, the random sampling model and the latent trait model. It is evident from the overview presented that there are some basic differences between the two models; there are also, however, some commonalities. Here we attempt to summarize both.

The basic assumption behind the R-S model is that the items that make up the test have been ramdomly sampled from a universe. To satisfy this assumption there must exist a well-defined universe of items as well as willingness to draw random samples from it. The feasibility of constructing a well-defined universe of items is in principle possible through the item-generation schemes discussed earlier.

The random sampling assumption can still be criticized on the grounds that users of achievement tests may not be willing to construct a test by random sampling, since often the determination of which items get included is dictated by pedagogical considerations. To some extent, such considerations can be accommodated by stratifying the universe of items by instructional objectives, for example, and then drawing a stratified random sample of items. Of course, if carried to an extreme, stratification may lead to a determined sample of items. In that case, there would seem to be very little difference from the traditional approach to constructing achievement tests, in which the judgment of the tester is used to decide which items get included in the test (Wood, 1976: 249).

If random sampling is the heart of the R-S model, unidimensionality and local independence are at the heart of the L-T model. These two concepts, however, are also important in the R-S model. Although unidimensionality and local independence are not explicitly mentioned in the context of the R-S model, they are still required to derive meaningful results from the R-S model. For example, the assumption in matrix sampling that the context in which the item occurs (i.e., what other items are included in the test) does not affect the response to the other items is another instance of the local independence assumptions.

The L-T model, however, instead of assuming random sampling, assumes that the relationship between performance on an item and achievement is known or can be estimated. The estimation is, of course, very dependent on unidimensionality and local independence, but the key consideration in the present context is what it takes to estimate the ICCs. Just as random sampling entails the existence of an item universe, the estimation of ICCs entails the availability of large amounts of data prior to the application of the model.

A more subtle implication, at least for achievement testing, is the need to consider when to estimate the ICCs. Since the trait being measured—achievement—is changing in level and even in the constituent psychological processes as a function of instruction, the time at which calibration is done is a crucial factor in the implementation of the L-T model to achievemet testing. This decision, in turn, seems to depend on the tester's views about the achievement process. If achievement is viewed as influenced by the same psychological processes, regardless of the content of instruction, then it would seem that calibration data could be collected either after each unit of instruction or after a series of units, since learning of subsequent units is not dependent on the knowledge of previous units. If, on the other hand, in addition to those psychological processes there is also an integrating or consolidation mechanism operating, it would seem that calibration data should be collected after a series of logically related instructional units.

Although the L-T model allows stronger results than the R-S model—for example, the existence of a local measure of precision of measurement—it is also true that these results are possible only through knowledge of the ICCs. As we have just seen, the time during instruction at which the calibration data are collected is an important consideration. Similarly, the conditions of administration affect, to some extent, the ICCs. For instance, if two random samples from some population take the same test—one under noisy, uncomfortable conditions and the other under quiet, comfortable conditions—the ICCs for a given item are likely to be different for the two groups. All of this suggests that an ICC is a "snapshot" of the relationship between performance and achievement at a particular point in time and space. As such, ICC theory is a static theory. By contrast, the R-S model is seemingly more dynamic, since it often concerns itself with variations in conditions of administration in order to estimate their influence (variance components) with respect to observed performance. That apparent dynamism of the R-S model, however, is valid within a single population. By contrast, the L-T model, even though it is static with respect to conditions of administration, is dynamic with respect to populations.

Another difference between the two models may be seen in their level of orientation. The R-S model is obviously total-test-score oriented, whereas the L-T model is item oriented. Within the R-S model, an item is viewed as a replication; within the L-T model, each item is an individual component with its own characteristics. Although it is not often done, those item characteristics may be thought of as dependent variables. It might, for example, be of interest to study an item's ICC in groups under different instructional strategies or under different administration procedures. More generally, generalizability theory can be brought to bear on the generalizability of ICCs. In such a case, items rather than persons are the subjects of study, and the item parameter estimates, rather than the estimated universe scores, are the dependent variables.

The item orientation of the L-T model is reflected in at least one more important way, namely the attention given, within the L-T model, to the "guessing problem." The L-T model, although it may not offer a solution agreeable to all (see Samejima, 1973), is at least cognizant of the problem. The R-S model, by contrast, does not formally recognize the problem. Similarly, the item orientation of the L-T model has led to the development of models beyond the dichotomous response level. In the R-S model, even though multiple response categories can be incorporated into the formulas, little advantage can be taken of the potential benefits accruing from recuperating partial knowledge through the use of multiple response categories.

4. THE ADMINISTRATION PROCEDURE

Almost all tests today are administered in a paper-and-pencil mode. That is, a group of testees gather to take the test, which has been previously printed in a booklet. Responses to each question are recorded on an answer sheet. Generally, everyone responds to the same set of questions, unless more than one form of the test is being administered for administrative reasons. This mode of test administration will be called "conventional."

Perhaps the major reason for the almost exclusive use of conventional testing is economy. It is relatively inexpensive to print tests. Costs may be reduced even further if the printed tests are reusable. The staff needed for administering a conventional test consists of at most a few monitors. Thus the cost of testing per testee is minimal. Although the cost effectiveness of the conventional procedure is undeniable, developments in psychometrics, computer science, and instructional psychology suggest that the time has come to reassess its usefulness.

Some of the psychometric developments surveyed in the foregoing sections are pertinent. Particularly significant is the development of algorithms for item generation; these make possible, at least in some content areas, the creation of items by computers. Also important in its implications for test administration is the development of psychometric theory to include the situation in which different testees are given different items, for both the L-T and R-S (nested case) models are capable of handling such testing situations. Within the R-S model this capability is exploited in the implementation of matrix and item sampling designs. The L-T model's capability is used to implement adaptive tests. Item sampling has already been discussed. In this section attention is focused on adaptive testing. Although the L-T model is not essential to adaptive testing, as shown by the work of several investigators (e.g., Cliff, 1975; Cliff et al., 1979), much of what follows is based on it.

A second line of development with implications for test administration was nurtured by advances in the computer field, most notably the increasing miniaturization of hardware coupled with corresponding reductions in cost. This trend suggests that in the not-too-distant future it may be possible to incorporate the computer routinely into the administration of tests. Indeed, plans are already under way to "computerize" the ASVAB (Armed Services Vocational Aptitude Battery), and a basic skills computer-based test is being developed at the Educational Testing Service.

Computer-Assisted Adaptive Testing

How can developments in psychometric theory and computer technology best be used in achievement testing, and what are the benefits of doing so? At a practical level, advantages of the computer administration of tests include better control over the security of the test, reduction in errors in transferring data on answer sheets to an analyzable form, more efficient storing of test data, and the possibility of immediate reports. All these advantages are important but would hardly justify computer administration from a purely psychometric point of view. The real advantage of computerized test administration lies in the possibility it furnishes of implementing new testing procedures that were not previously feasible. In addition, computer administration allows and facilitates the implementation of response modes other than multiple-choice. Although the display capabilities of computer-based testing systems have been limited, it is currently possible to present items in a different format—for example, free response (Vale, 1977). Also, because of the continuing enhancements of the display capabilities of computer terminals, it is now possible to present highly graphic items.

From a psychometric point of view, there are two distinct advantages to computer administration. One is increased precision of measurement; the other is a more controlled testing environment. To the extent that these advantages improve the validity of test scores, it may be argued that computerized testing is capable of breaking the existing "plateau" in validity of conventional testing. These two central advantages of computerized testing go back at least to Binet (see Weiss, 1973). Because of the nature of his intelligence test and the population he tested, Binet found it necessary to administer the instrument on an individual basis. It must have become obvious after a short while that there was no point in administering the entire test to every individual. Instead, it was more efficient, and psychologically more judicious, to limit the test to those items that were "appropriate" in difficulty for a given individual. This is precisely what computerized adaptive testing is all about: constructing a test tailored to each individual test taker. The tailoring is done by the computer on a sequential basis; that is, what item is administered next depends on the testee's performance either on the previous item or on all previsou items. The procedures for this tailoring are called *adaptive testing strategies*. In this section I will describe some of these strategies, then turn to a review of the literature evaluating these strategies.

A classification of testing strategies. In an excellent review, McBride (1979) suggested a three-faceted classification scheme for adaptive testing. The first facet, item pool structure, distinguishes between strategies that require the pool of items to be ordered in some fashion (for example, stratified by difficulty level) and strategies that do not require such arrangements. The second facet, item selection algorithms, distinguishes between ways of choosing the next item. Mechanical strategies choose the next item on the basis of the response to the previous items; mathematical strategies, on the other hand, use the information in all previously administered items. Finally, the third facet distinguishes between strategies of administering the same number of items to each testee and strategies of allowing testees to take a different number of items. It is beyond the scope of this work to describe each strategy that may be obtained from the crossing of these three facets. Instead, I will describe those that have been used most often in empirical research.

Two-stage adaptive testing. Of all adaptive testing strategies, the two-stage test is closest to conventional administration, since in essence it consists of two conventional tests. The first is called the routing test and serves to assign testees to one of several achievement levels. Once a classification is made, the testee is administered a second test appropriate to his or her level of achievement. The testee's performances on the routing test and the second test are used for scoring purposes. That not all students responded to the same items presents no problems within an L-T framework. It should be pointed out that two-stage strategy does not require the L-T model. Cronbach and Gleser (1965) discussed the idea from a decision-theory point of view.

Lord (1980b) discussed two-stage tests within the L-T model. To illustrate the myriad variables that enter into the design of even a very simple strategy, consider the following parameters identified by Lord:

(1) the total number of items given to a single examinee;
(2) the number of available second-stage tests;
(3) the number of alternative responses per item;
(4) the number of items in the routing or first-stage test;
(5) the difficulty level of the routing test;
(6) the method of scoring the routing test;
(7) the cut-off point on the routing test that determines which second-stage test an examinee will take;
(8) the difficulty level of the second-stage test;
(9) the method of scoring the combined items from the first- and second-stage tests.

Because of the large number of variables, it is not possible to arrive analytically at the "best" design. In any case, many of the variables could be fixed a priori by the constraints of the situation. For instance, the number of alternatives per item is often not controllable by the psychometrician. Instead, there is usually an existing pool of items of, say, five alternatives each. Nevertheless, in an attempt to arrive at some guidelines, Lord (1971) conducted extensive Monte-Carlo experiments. He noted (1980b) that, compared to up-and-down procedures (which themselves are not optimal), the two-stage procedure left something to be desired in measurement accuracy at the extreme level of ability, when guessing was assumed present. A further problem with two-stage procedures is that a certain proportion of testees will be misclassified by the routing tests and will end up taking an inappropriate second-stage test.

Even though two-stage testing may not be optimal, unlike most other adaptive testing strategies, it need not be administered by computer (see Fischer and Pendl, 1980; de Gruijter, 1980). In fact, it has now been implemented in STEP III, a commercial test distributed by Educational Testing Service. As implemented in STEP III, the routing test consists of a fifteen-item test. Depending on the score, the student is then given one of three second-stage tests.

The flexilevel strategy. The flexilevel strategy was proposed by Lord (1971). It is an instance of a strategy requiring a structured item pool, mechanical branching, and a fixed test length. If the test length is k, then a pool containing (2k – 1) items is required. The strategy calls for administering first the item of median difficulty and then the (k – 1) contiguous item that are most appropriate in difficulty for a given individual. Suppose k = 5; this means the pool must contain nine items. The easiest sequence of five items would consist of the five easiest items; the hardest sequence would consist of the five hardest items. One of the most attractive features of the flexilevel test is that it need not be administered by computer. It is possible by means of special answer sheets to administer it in a "paper-and-pencil" mode. However, Olivier (1974) found that many students were unable to follow the complex instructions. The flexilevel test is discussed further by Lord (1980a). Empirical investigations have been carried out by Betz and Weiss (1975), Harris and Pennell (1977), and Seguin (1976).

The stradaptive strategy. This strategy was suggested by Weiss (1973) and has been one of the most researched strategies (see Weiss, 1974). It is an instance of a structured item pool and mechanical branching; the termination, however, may be variable or fixed.

The item pool is arranged into a number of nonoverlapping strata—usually nine—of increasing difficulty. Within a stratum, items are usually ordered in decreasing discrimination. Therefore, the most discriminating items in the pool would be administered first by the procedure. The first administered item is determined from prior information about the individual. If the first item is from strategy m, the next item will be from strategy (m + 1) (the next most difficult stratum) if the first item is answered correctly. If the item has been answered incorrectly, then the next item is from stratum (m − 1). Figure 2 shows a typical response protocol. This particular student performs at a high level, as seen by the tendency to be administered items of high difficulty.

Maximum-likelihood and Bayesian strategies. Maximum likelihood and Bayesian strategies are instances of the use of a mathematical procedure to select the next item. The fundamental idea is to choose as the next item the item that yields maximum information, given the student's current estimate of achievement. The idea in Owen's (1975) Bayesian procedure is similar, but instead of maximizing information, the objective is to minimize the variance of the posterior distribution of θ. A Bayesian procedure has been recently implemented on microcomputers (Bock and Mislevy, 1982) with apparent success.

In practical testing situations it is unlikely that items will be chosen with the sole purpose of maximizing information or minimizing posterior variance. Instead, other characteristics of the items are taken into consideration. For example, it may be important to administer items from each of several content areas, or to administer different items in a certain proportion. Lord's (1977b) broad range test implements some of these constraints.

Evaluation of
Adaptive Achievement Testing

Although there seems to be unanimous agreement that adaptive testing is, in principle, a good idea, its empirical evaluation has proved difficult in practice; for reviews, see Weiss (1973), Wood (1973), McBride (1979), and Kreitzberg et al. (1978). On the whole, however, the research suggests that adaptive testing is superior to conventional paper-and-pencil testing in that it measures more precisely over a wider range of performance levels. Nevertheless, for several reasons, the existing research is less than adequate in evaluating the usefulness of achievement testing.

Much of the research is based on simulation and analytical results. Monte Carlo and analytical evaluations of adaptive testing are to some extent misleading, since they assume that the latent trait model fits

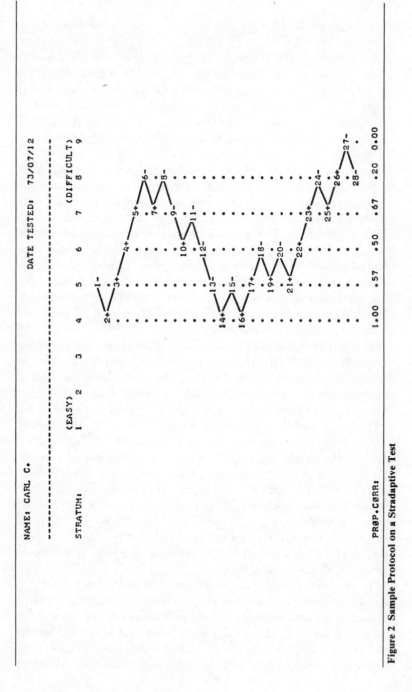

Figure 2 Sample Protocol on a Stradaptive Test

responses obtained under the adaptive procedure. The problem is best appreciated by examining the procedure of fitting the model (e.g., estimating parameters) to a pool of items. One procedure would consist of administering a previously calibrated test along with the to-be-calibrated items. Since the number of items that can be given to any sample of testees is limited, additional samples would be required to calibrate the entire pool. The fact that all samples responded to a set of common items allows the estimations of the uncalibrated items on a common metric. Eventually all the items are mixed in a pool and administered by computer. When an item finally appears on the screen of the computer terminal, there is no guarantee that responses to it can be accurately modeled using the previously obtained parameters, since the context in which the item appeared at calibration time is very different from the context in which it appeared in the adaptive test and since there is reason to believe (e.g., Yen, 1980; Whiteley and Dawis, 1976) that such context effects are strong. In an adaptive test, not only are the surrounding items different but so is the medium of presentation. In addition, feedback is often given as part of the computerized administration; this raises the possibility of violations of the local independence assumption (see Gialluca and Weiss, 1980).

Beyond these situational factors in achievement testing (unlike in ability testing), the relation between performance and the trait is bound to change as a function of time. For example, as instruction takes place, a student is likely to see new connections among concepts; thus the learning of new concepts may consolidate the understanding of earlier concepts. The implication of all this for achievement testing is that we must keep in mind that item parameter estimates and achievement estimates are, strictly speaking, valid for only a single point in time.

It is reasonable to expect that the proper time for calibration of items occurs immediately after instruction in a series of interdependent content areas has been completed, for this would tend to ensure the unidimensionality assumption. An extreme violation of this principle would consist of calibrating the items before and after instruction. Kingsbury and Weiss (1979) found that the ICCs at pretest time were quite different from the ICCs after instruction.

The net effect of all these circumstances on the relationship of achievement to performance is hard to predict. However, let us assume that parameters change proportionately in such a way that the "true" information function is raised or lowered by a constant at all achievement levels. If the true information function is in fact higher, then the actual level of information attained by the adaptive procedure will have been underestimated. On the other hand, if the true information is lower, the the actual level of information extracted by the adaptive procedure will have been overestimated. If the parameters change in a more complicated fashion, it is more difficult to analyze the situation, but it seems clear that the efficiency of the adaptive procedure must be eroded, since the branching would have been done on inappropriate parameter and ability estimates.

The Validity of
Adaptive Achievement Testing

From a pragmatic point of view, the ultimate triumph or defeat of adaptive testing is not likely to depend on how much information it extracts (i.e., reliability) but rather on validity considerations. In attempting such validation studies it should be recalled that validity, (defined as the correlation with a criterion) is certain to decrease if the adaptive test functions as it should. In other words, since adaptive tests are more reliable, they must correlate to a lesser extent with a criterion unless both the adaptive test and the criterion are congeneric (e.g., Bejar, forthcoming d). These considerations suggest that a more defensible approach to the validation of adaptive testing, and educational measurement in general, is construct validation. See Messick (1975) for a discussion of construct validation of educational measures.

An example of this approach to validation is seen in Bejar and Weiss (1978). They postulated a nomological net to account for achievement in a biology college course and proceeded to test its feasibility by means of a structural equation model. (See Bentler [1978] for a discussion of construct validation by means of structural equation models.) The net is seen in Figure 3. The rectangles represent observable variables; the circles represent the construct postulated to account for the interrelationships among the six observable variables. The coefficients next to the arrows are those that need to be estimated. The direction of the arrow indicates that the variable at the head of the arrow is regressed on the variable at the other end of the arrow. This approach thus permits an evaluation of adaptive achievement testing in the context of an instructionally significant model. From this point of view, the most relevant information from this model is the difference between the (standardized) regression coefficients of the adaptive and classroom test on the postulated construct. Although no major difference was found in this respect, the adaptive test scores were based on about 25% fewer items. This suggests that adaptive testing can substantially decrease testing time without jeopardizing the overall validity of the test.

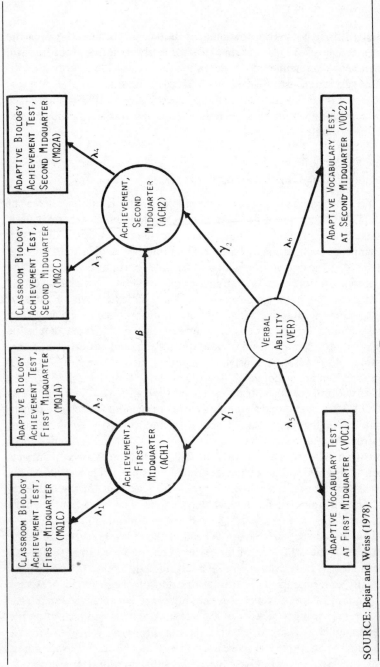

SOURCE: Bejar and Weiss (1978).

Figure 3 Nomological Net for Validation of Adaptive Achievement Test

Summary

Both theoretical and empirical results suggest that adaptive testing could be an efficient and valid approach to the measurement of achievement. However, further research is clearly needed to pinpoint, in terms of relevant criteria, how useful it really is in practical situations. For example, since most of the work in this area is based on the L-T model, more thought needs to be given to the empirical and conceptual feasibility of the unidimensionality assumption in an achievement context (see Bejar, 1983; Traub, 1983). To the extent, however, that the assumptions are met, we may expect to derive benefits from adaptive achievement testing beyond increases in the precision of measurement. For example, the problem of out-of-level testing (e.g., Long et al., 1977) may be relieved by an adaptive testing system; better evaluation of large educational programs may be possible (Bejar, 1980b). Finally and perhaps most important, adaptive achievement testing may permit a closer integration of instruction and assessment.

5. INTERPRETATIONS AND DECISIONS BASED ON ACHIEVEMENT TEST SCORES

The two most common current approaches for interpreting test scores are, with respect to norms, so-called norm-referenced testing (NRT), and with respect to a "criterion," so-called criterion-referenced testing (CRT). Norm-referenced test scores are scaled with respect to the variability of observed performance in the norming group. In the CRT approach there is less interest in an individual's relative standing; rather, the intent is to describe in concrete terms what an individual can do. Thus, Glaser and Nitko (1971: 653) defined a criterion-referenced test as "one that is deliberately constructed to yield measurements that are directly interpretable in terms of specified performance standards."

The last several years have seen a growing controversy between NRT and CRT, but the basis of the controversy has not always been clear. The controversy culminated in a presidential debate sponsored by the American Educational Research Association. Perhaps the most illuminating distinction was drawn by Ebel (1979), who suggested that the key to the difference between NRT and CRT lies in their differing instructional philosophies:

If the primary goals of learning are to acquire a series of essential abilities, distinct enough from each other, few enough in number, and important enough individually to be specified separately, studied separately, and mastered separately, then a criterion-referenced test is clearly the test that ought to be used. But if the substance of learning is an infinity of particulars, too numerous to be specified separately, too inter-dependent to be studied or mastered separately; if the goal of learning lies beyond acquisition to understanding; and if understanding results from coming to know the multitude of relationships among these particulars, then a test that probes for these relationships at as many different points and from as many different angles as possible is the kind of test that ought to be used. Such a test is now commonly referred to as a norm-referenced test [Ebel, 1979: 4].

Failure to recognize this distinction led Popham to suggest that NRT tests "are essentially worthless," when at worst NRTs are not optimal under certain instructional models. For example, Rosner (1975) assumed that certain "perceptual skills" facilitate learning in reading and mathematics, and he designed a curriculum to teach these skills. An integral part of that curriculum was a series of CRTs designed to determine whether a student had mastered the different skills. In this case there is no point in trying to interpret performance with respect to norms, since the object of instruction is to ready each individual to undertake further instructions. The object of assessment is in this case to detect whether the necessary skills have been acquired.

Popham (1978) also claimed that there is a real difference between NRT and CRT in terms of their construction. However, the most basic ingredient of an achievement testing system is the creation of an item pool in which performance can largely be explained in terms of exposure to instruction. This should be the objective of an achievement test, regardless of whether scores are to be interpreted with respect to norms or criteria. In this sense there is only one kind of achievement test, namely, one that is valid for its intended application. The deficits Popham identified in NRT, such as teaching-testing mismatches, are not necessarily characteristic of NRT but, rather, illustrate instances of less-than-optimal utilization of tests. In short, it seems that there are no real differences between NRT and CRT with respect to the psychometric principles behind the two. Within the R-S model both absolute (CRT) and differential (NRT) interpretations of test scores coexist happily. Within the L-T model the distinction is not even recognized and leaves interpretation entirely to the user. Indeed, Hambleton (1983) has applied the L-T model to criterion-referenced tests.

Dynamic Interpretation
of Achievement Test Scores

Although the interpretations of scores with respect to norms and criteria are the most common ones, they are by no means the only ones. Their dominance is due to their affinity with two major schools of psychology. NRT emanates from the differential psychology tradition and thus emphasizes differences among individuals. On the other hand, CRT comes from a behavioristic tradition and thus emphasizes what an individual can do. In a sense, both interpretations leave something to be desired. A purely NRT or CRT interpretation is a static one, a characteristic that is at odds with the dynamic nature of achievement. Thus, not only is it informative to know how much the testees know or what they can do, but also how much they have learned since the last testing. That is, how much more do they now know relative to the last testing, and what can they now do that they were not able to do at the last testing. However, the measurement of change implied by this approach to achievement presents practical problems.

The reason for this lies in the psychometric difficulties associated with measuring change. These difficulties were outlined in Harris (1963). Since then, Linn and Slinde (1977) have provided an updated review of the literature and have concluded along with Cronbach and Furby (1970) that the best way to measure change is by rephrasing the question so as to avoid the estimation of change. More concretely, according to Cronbach and Snow (1977: 116)

> Outcomes in learning research, especially educational research, then, ought to be expressed in terms of level scores collected at some terminal point (and perhaps at intermediate points also). In evaluating those results, one will have to take the varying initial status of learners into account, usually by making it a covariate. The reliability of these measures will, of course, be limited by the chance character of many events during learning.

To a large extent, the difficulties with the measurement of change are rooted on the presence of sizable errors of measurement. So far, however, these difficulties have been demonstrated in the context of the R-S model and its specialization into the classical model. It becomes relevant to ask whether the difficulties would vanish in the context of the L-T model.

Problems with change scores. One of the key problems with the measurement of change is the unreliability of change scores (Bereiter,

1963; Linn and Slinde, 1977). According to Bereiter, the typically low reliability of change scores is due to the unreliability of the pretest and posttest. The reliability of change scores can be increased either by lowering the correlation between pre and post and/or by improving the reliability of pre and post. Clearly, of the two choices, the latter is more appealing, as one could hardly justify a low correlation between achievement at two points in time. But how can the reliability of the pretest and posttest be increased? One way is by means of computer-assisted administration procedures. Some of those procedures were discussed in the preceding section. It appears, however, that only those schemes that rely on the L-T model are likely to be maximally useful for this purpose, since they allow monitoring of the precision of measurement. In this sense, the L-T model could provide a solution to a long-standing psychometric problem.

Another longstanding problem in the measurement of change is the establishment of a well-defined metric along which an individual's progress can be charged (Linn and Slinde, 1977). The problem arises because, if instruction is effective, at least some testees will "hit the ceiling" if the posttest is of the same difficulty as the pretest. As a result, the change measure will not be accurate for those individuals: It will be an underestimate.

A potential solution to this problem within the R-S model is to devise a universe of items with a wide difficulty range so as to prevent students' reaching the ceiling even after extended periods of instruction. Although this would put repeated measures on the same metric of necessity, each score is likely to be fairly unreliable, since tests taken at random from the universe will have widely distributed difficulties rather than concentrated on a difficulty range, which is necessary to increase precision of measurement.

An alternative solution is to stratify the universe of items by difficulty levels and administer tests sampled from increasingly more difficult strata as instruction goes on. This solution might improve to some extent the unreliability of scores, but the scores from each stratum would not be on the same metric and would not be comparable. To put such scores on the same metric it is necessary to vertically equate the strata. However, as Slinde and Linn (1978) have shown, equating procedures based on the classical model are less than adequate for this purpose. The difficulty is largely due to the fact that universe scores from strata differing in difficulty have a nonlinear relationship, a fact that introduces a variety of technical problems. By contrast, within the L-T model vertical equating is a "linear problem" (Lord, 1977c); however, Slinde and Linn (1978), have found that one-parameter models were not optimal for this purpose (but see Slinde and Linn, 1979). They concluded that two- or three-parameter models might be necessary.

Measuring achievement curves. For simplicity we have focused our attention so far on the measurement of change involving a pretest and a posttest. The general problem is, of course, the measurement of growth or achievement curves across several points in time. Growth curves have received recent attention (e.g., Bock, 1976; Fischer, 1980; Ragosa et al., 1982; Sanathanan, 1980).

Bock (1976) has proposed an L-T model that could be used for measuring achievement curves. The model contains several ingredients. The psychometric scheme is based on a two-parameter normal ogive model. The calibration of the model requires the availability of testees who have undergone increasing amounts of instruction but who are otherwise comparable. The unique feature of the procedure is that it ensures a well-defined metric by assigning mean achievement to the different groups in such a way as to maximize the fit of the normal ogive simultaneously across groups. In fact, Bock seems to view this part of the model as a means of obtaining scores with a well-defined metric. He has argued, however, that the precision of measurement of each score will not be sufficiently high to make firm determinations as to the shape of the achievement curve. His solution is to supplement the psychometric model with a statistical model that assigns the individuals to a particular growth pattern. Having assigned an individual to a growth pattern, the next step is to estimate the individual's growth parameters. For instance, if an individual is assigned a linear classification, then his growth parameter is the slope, (i.e., rate of achievement parameters). According to Bock (1976: 80), the statistical portion of the model has an important purpose:

> Despite the best efforts of psychometric research, it is difficult to be optimistic of increasing the reliability of educational and behavior measures sufficiently to permit a similar purely empirical approach to the measurement of individual change—that is, an approach that attempts to determine, from the data, the time-dependent change in the measure without prior constraints on the functional form of change.

From an achievement-testing point of view (and in all fairness, it should be stated that Bock proposed the model as a developmental one) the need or utility of the statistical part of the model can be questioned on two grounds. First, making decisions about an individual based partly on collateral information, as Bock proposed, seems questionable for the reasons discussed earlier in connection with estimates of universe scores. Second, the assertion that we have reached a plateau with respect to precision of measurement is true only with respect to *conventional* testing procedures. Adaptive testing has the potential to minimize and equalize precision of measurement at all levels of achievement. How much precision is obtained depends on the characteristics of the item pool. It remains an empirical question whether the available quality in existing item pools, coupled with adaptive testing, can provide sufficient precision to adequately measure achievement without using collateral information.

Mastery Testing

While relatively little has been done in the area of measuring growth, there is a growing literature on mastery testing. Mastery testing can be conceived as a special case of growth measurement, in which the objective is to detect the surpassing of a certain threshold of achievement. Mastery testing can be viewed as a pedagogical concept and separately as a psychometric concept. From a psychometric point of view, mastery testing is simply a procedure for determining whether an individual has attained a certain level of performance. As a pedagogical concept (e.g., Block, 1971) mastery testing is based on Carroll's (1963) model of school learning. In that model achievement is viewed as being influenced by a number of factors, such as motivation and quality of instruction. However, only one factor—time—has been emphasized by proponents of mastery testing (e.g., Bloom, 1974). According to Bloom, if given enough time, most students can attain a certain level of achievement. This instructional model has hardly gone uncriticized (e.g., Greeno, 1978), but it is not within the scope of this work to discuss those criticisms. In this section I will simply review some basic concepts of decision theory and see how they are applied within the R-S and L-T model to the problem of deciding whether a given testee has achieved mastery.

Some elements of decision theory applied to mastery testing. According to Lindgren (1971), decision making in general involves four elements:

(a) a set of possible actions from which one must choose,
(b) the circumstances that prevail,

(c) consequences from taking a given action in the fact of a given set of circumstances, and

(d) data.

In mastery decisions there are two possible actions—assign to mastery category; do not assign to mastery category. The circumstances that could prevail are whether the individual has in fact achieved mastery or not. The third ingredient involves the gains or losses associated with every combination of actions and circumstances. The last ingredient is, in our case, the test score for a given individual.

The first three ingredients can be represented in terms of a 2×2 table:

	Δ_1	Δ_2
d_1	0	1
d_2	2	0

wherein d_1 and d_2 are the possible actions (d_1 = do not assign to mastery, d_2 = assign to mastery). The possible prevailing circumstances are Δ_1 and Δ_2 (Δ_1 = the individual has not achieved mastery; Δ_2 = the individual has achieved mastery). The consequences are represented in this table as losses. Thus, if we assign a master to mastery or a nonmaster to nonmastery we lose nothing. On the other hand, if we incorrectly assign a master to the nonmastery category or a nonmaster to the mastery category we incur losses. For illustration we assume that latter error is twice as serious as the former error.

It is possible now to compute the expected loss associated with all conceivable decision rules. In the present example there are three possible decision rules.

(1) Assign to mastery, regardless of the score, x.
(2) Assign to nonmastery, regardless of the score, x.
(3) Assign to mastery if $x > \epsilon$; or assign to nonmasery if $x < \epsilon$, where ϵ is some cutoff score.

Davis and associates (1973) outlines a three-step procedure for arriving at decisions based on the loss table and the set of possible decisions. The first step is to compute the expected loss for each (d, Δ) combination for each of the decision rules. The expectations is taken with respect to the probabilities $p_1 = p(x \geq \epsilon | \Delta_1)$ and $p_2 = p(x < \epsilon | \Delta_2)$. Here p_1 is the probability that a student who has achieved mastery scores at or above a cutoff score ϵ, and p_2 is the probability that a student who has not achieved mastery scores below that cutoff score.

For a given decision rule the expected loss is

$$\text{Expected loss} = (d_1, \Delta_1)p_1 + (d_2, \Delta_1)(1 - p_1)$$

if Δ_1 prevails and

$$(d_1, \Delta_2)p_2 + (d_2, \Delta_2)(1 - p_2)$$

if Δ_2 prevails.

After performing this computation for each of the decision rules it is possible to determine which decision rule minimizes the loss. If the proportion of students that have achieved mastery is known, or if one is willing to assume it known, then it is possible to weight the expected loss associated with Δ_1 by the proportion of students who have achieved mastery and to weight the expected loss associated with Δ_2 by the proportion of students who have not achieved mastery. The resulting weighted expected loss is the Bayes risk function. The decision rule yielding the least Bayes risk would be chosen as the best decision.

Davis et al. (1973) referred to this procedure as "normal form analysis." A second procedure—called "extensive form analysis"—leads to the same conclusions and offers certain computational advantages. The approach is illustrated by Swaminathan et al. (1975). An important difference is that while the normal form analysis relies on the conditional probability $p(x|\Delta)$, the extensive form analysis relies on the conditional probability $p(\Delta|x)$. The conditional probabilities may be obtained by a variety of procedures. Some of these are reviewed by Swaminatham et al. (1975). The procedure they favor is based on Bayesian considerations; i.e., they incorporate collateral information into the estimation of those probabilities.

The above scheme can easily be applied within the L-T model. Let mastery be defined such that if $\theta \geq \theta_0$ the individual is a master, and a nonmaster otherwise. If we use the extensive form approach we need to compute the probability $p(\Delta|x)$, that is, the probability of mastery given the observed score, or $p(\theta_a > \theta_0 | \hat{\theta}_a)$. We know that at least asymptotically the distribution of $\hat{\theta}_a$ is normal with mean θ_a and variance $1/I(\theta_a)$. Therefore, we can estimate the probability of exceeding the cutoff given the estimated θ by

$$p = \frac{1}{\sqrt{2\pi}} \int_{-\infty}^{z} e^{-t^2/2} dt$$

where

$$z = (\hat{\theta}_a - \theta_o)/\sqrt{I} \; (\hat{\theta}_a)$$

If θ_a is estimated by means of a Bayesian procedure such as Owen's, then the probability can be found by reference to a normal distribution using as a denominator the square root of the variance of the posterior distributions instead of $I(\hat{\theta}_a)$. A more detailed procedure for applying the L-T model to a mastery situation is described by Lord (1980a); see also Vale, 1977).

Determination of cutoff scores. Perhaps the most significant issue surrounding mastery testing is the derivation of the cutoff point. Several procedures have been suggested and can roughly be classified into analytical procedures—such as those proposed by Emrick (1971) and Hambleton and Novick (1973)—and judgmental procedures—such as those proposed by Nedelsky (1954) and Angoff (1971). Glass (1978) described the various approaches in the context of a larger discussion about the proper role of standards. He argued that the determination of mastery (i.e., the cutoff) must ultimately be arbitrary and must therefore be avoided, since it has no foundation in psychology, nor is it possible to obtain agreement among judges. He suggested that the solution to the problem lies in abandoning mastery decisions and judging achievement not by comparison to standards but by assessing change:

> Perhaps the only criterion that is safe and convincing in education is change. Increases in cognitive performance are generally regarded as good, decreases as bad. Although one cannot make satisfactory judgments of performance (Is this level of reading performance good or masterful?), one can readily judge an improvement in performance as good and a decline as bad [Glass, 1978: 259].

In practice, of course, decisions must be made and cutoffs must be determined.

Dependability of mastery decisions. When test scores are used to make dichotomous decisions, psychometric characteristics such as generalizability and information are not as useful, since they pertain to test scores. A variety of procedures have been suggested for assessing the reliability of mastery decisions, but Kane and Brennan (1980) have been able to formulate a general framework that subsumes many of these suggestions, including procedures that postulate threshold loss functions, such as those proposed by Huyhn (1976), Subkoviak (1976),

Swaminathan et al. (1974), and procedures which postulate a squared-error loss function such as those proposed by Livingston (1972). In addition, they define dependability in terms of the expected agreement among randomly selected instances of the testing procedure and therefore do not require the more stringent assumption about the existence of parallel forms.

Theoretical Interpretations
of Test Scores

It was pointed out above that criterion- and norm-referenced interpretations were static in the sense of not attempting to measure change. Both interpretations are static also in the sense of being unconcerned with the cognitive processes that mediate performance. To the extent that achievement testing theory should dovetail with instructional theory, it would be most awkward to ignore such cognitive processes, since they are playing an increasingly large role in instructional psychology (see Wittrock and Lumsdaine, 1977). In what follows, three important validation schemes that attempt to integrate psychological and measurement theory will be discussed.

Taxonomic approaches. One of the earliest attempts to place achievement testing within a formal framework was the work initiated at the University of Chicago by Ralph Tyler and Benjamin Bloom, which has come to be known as "Bloom's taxonomy." The general approach taken by this group was to conceive of two facets for classifying items. One facet was behavioral, i.e., based on the content matter; the other facet was cognitive, i.e., what psychological functions are required to answer the item. Travers (1980) has strongly criticized the taxonomy, arguing that it fails to provide a useful scheme for conceiving achievement (although he did not deny that the scheme is probably useful as a means of classifying items). Travers argued that the proponents of the taxonomy believed in the existence of categories waiting to be discovered and, like others before them, did not achieve a useful product:

> Lavoisier in chemistry and Lamarck in biology, recognized that classes with highest utility were *not* out there existing in the real world—but were constructions of scientists searching for ways of understanding empirical data [Travers 1980: 16].

Travers argued that what the developers of the taxonomy found was just a set of customs "that had slowly evolved for convenience in the pedagogical arts," rather than a classification of fundamental importance. As for the cognitive mechanisms postulated, Travers argued that they were not sufficiently defined to be really useful. Based on this analysis, it does not appear that the so-called Bloom taxonomy can provide a solid foundation for the validation of achievement tests.

Hierarchical approaches. A sounder foundation for achievement could be built from work on learning hierarchies. Unlike the taxonomic approach, which is more appropriate for cataloging items, the rationale of learning hierarchies is sequencing instructions. A learning hierarchy may be thought of as a statement of the prerequisite skills of competent performance. For example, in the case of two skills, a simple learning hierarchy hypothesizes that C1 must be learned before C2.

Learning hierarchies were first investigated by Gagné (Gagné and Paradise, 1961, Gagné et al., 1962; Gagné et al., 1965). Although the cognitive mechanisms that underlie performance are not generally identified by the proponents of a learning hierarchy, the postulation of a hierarchy is consistent with construct validity since the validation of the hierarchy rests on response consistency, as shown below. In the two-skill example, if C1 is supposed to precede C2, then in principle the only two admissible response vectors are

C1	C2
1	1
1	0

That is, the student is expected to acquire both skills or only the most elementary one. Instances of students acquiring skill B but not A contradict the learning hierarchy. The early investigations conducted by Gagné were suggestive of the validity of learning hierarchies postulated, but they suffered from certain methodological weaknesses (see White, 1973). Some of these problems were failing to take error of measurement into account, misspecifying components of the hierarchy, and delay of testing; that is, the hierarchy was tested at the completion of instruction, thus permitting the introduction of forgetting. Also, the items used to assess mastery may not have been fully homogeneous.

White suggested a more rigorous approach to validation of learning hierarchies. In the case of a simple two-component hierarchy—say, C1 and C2—the procedure requires that a group of students who have not mastered C2 be assigned randomly to two instructional conditions. One condition teaches C2 and then C1, the other condition teaches C1 only. The results of such an experiment can be recorded as follows:

Possible Response Vectors After Instruction (1 = mastery)		Relative Frequencies of Response Vectors Within Each Instructional Condition	
Mastered C1	Mastered C2	C2 then C1	C1 only
1	1	f_{11}	f_{12}
0	1	f_{21}	f_{22}
1	0	f_{31}	f_{32}
0	0	f_{41}	f_{42}

Several analyses could be performed on such data, but White's discussion concentrates on f_{31}. For the hierarchy to be validated, the frequency of the response vector $\{1\ 0\}$ should be 0, in principle. In practice, one is likely to compare f_{31} and f_{32} and hope to find, if the hierarchy is valid, that f_{31} is far smaller than f_{32}.

As White (1973) noted, this approach may be impractical for large hierarchies. More practical procedures have been discussed by Airasian and Bart (1975) and McCready (1975), and more recently by Rindskopf (1983). These authors essentially propose statistical methodologies to test the agreement of the postulated hierarchy to data.

Cognitive Approaches

One characteristic of learning hierarchies research is the omission of mention of the cognitive mechanism that may underlie the acquisition of knowledge. Once a learning hierarchy is validated, such knowledge would appear unnecessary. It is likely, however, that for some students the skills are not optimally acquired in the prescribed order. For example, some students may not master the highest skills within a reasonable period of time, nor do they proceed through the hierarchy at the same speed. To explain such differences, we are likely to resort to explanations that involve unobservable variables, i.e., hypothetical constructs. The identification of these variables is likely to be useful in designing methods of instruction that would allow the slower students to proceed faster and thus master higher skills in a shorter period of time. This seems to require an understanding of the cognitive mechanisms underlying learning. If such knowledge is important to understanding learning, it would also seem important to understanding tests. This calls for cognitively oriented construct validation of test scores.

Construct validation of achievement test scores. In much of the psychological measurement literature, construct validity (Cronbach and Meehl, 1955) is the ultimate goal. In achievement testing, on the other hand, construct validity has had a very limited role (Messick,

1975). Instead, according to Messick, content validity is the primary concern in much of achievement testing. This position is clearly exemplified in Shoemaker's (1975) requirement that the item pool and instruction be closely related to each other. A similar position is held by Guttman (1969, 1980), who is a strong advocate of an achievement-test theory based on content. The contrasting position has been eloquently stated by Messick, who has argued that content validity is a *necessary* component of achievement testing, but not a *sufficient* one. Attention must also be given to the process that generates the response to the items, i.e. construct validity. To infer the nature of that process it is necessary to examine responses to the items:

> Inferences in educational and psychological measurement are made from scores, and scores are a function of subject responses. Any concept of validity of measurement must include reference to empirical consistency. Content coverage is an important consideration in test construction and interpretation, to be sure, but in itself it does not provide validity [Messick, 1975: 960].

Messick's call for construct validity in achievement testing comes at a time when instructional and educational psychology is undergoing transformation from the earlier behavioristic bent to a cognitive one. In a recent review of the literature, Wittrock and Lumsdaine (1977) made the following remarks:

> The current shift emphasizes the study of central cognitive and affective associationistic and holistic processes by which the learner selects, transforms, and encodes the nominal characteristics of experience into functional, meaningful internal representations. *A cognitive perspective implies that a behavioral analysis of instruction is often inadequate to explain the effects of instruction upon learning.* From a cognitive perspective, to understand the effects of instruction upon learning and memory one must comprehend how learners use their cognitive processes, knowledge, abilities, aptitudes, and interests to transform the nominal stimuli of instruction into functional ones. These cognitive processes include attention, motivation, verbal and imaginal encoding, storage, and retrieval. The shift helps to bring together experimental psychology and differential psychology [1977: 418; italics added].

The dichotomy between content and process has the potential for creating acrimonious debates (see Tenopyr, 1977) between proponents of the two points of view. Fortunately, however, the validity of both points of view is being recognized and integrated. Glaser (1976: 12) commented on the distinction:

> As suggested by the above examples, the work on the analysis of competent performance that is going on at the present time is of two kinds: the characterization of the information structures and cognitive processes of the skilled performer and behaviorally oriented work on rational task analysis. Such analyses of human competence and subject-matter tasks may allow us to do two things regarding the optimization of instruction: (a) Specifying the structures and processes by which competent individuals might be performing a task may put us in a position to try to teach these processes to individual learners. (b) Knowing that a task is performed efficiently in one way rather than in another might enable us to design instruction so that the performance learned allows individuals to directly or indirectly transfer to the more efficient method.

In short, based on the development we have surveyed, this would seem a propitious time to incorporate construct validity as an important dimension of achievement tests. As noted in Nitko's review (1980: 479), even criterion-referenced tests can be profitably validated from that perspective.

How does one go about construct validating an achievement test? How shoud we choose among constructs, and by what methodology should we assess validity? It is beyond the aim of this effort to formulate a construct-validation methodology for achievement tests. However, such methodology is likely to include the integration of content and processes.

Messick (1981), in discussing this point, noted that for content validity the test development strategy calls for an identification of the behavioral domain by reference to curriculum objectives. This step has two components—content relevance and content coverage (Messick, 1981). Content relevance refers to the rules that define whether a given item is a member of the universe of items. Content coverage refers to the rules for sampling items from the universe of items in a representative fashion.

A construct validation approach requires, in addition to substantive coverage, response consistency. Moreover, according to Messick (1981) (see also Tenopyr, 1977) substantive coverage and response consistency are interdependent considerations. That is, we cannot have construct validity unless both substantive coverage and response consistency are present. At the item level a construct validation approach requires planting in the test items that do not belong to the universe—that is, that are not valid from a substantive point of view. If responses to the content-invalid items can be explained by the same construct that explains response to the content-valid items, we have failed to show construct validity. In short, construct validity, far from ignoring content validity, strengthens it by requiring response consistency.

Response consistency can best be defined in relation to psychometric response models. The two major models (R-S and L-T) were discussed in a previous section. In general, the choice of model is independent of whether the achievement testing system has a construct or content orientation. However, it appears that the latent trait model is more useful at the item level, since it explicitly deals with the issue of dimensionality, i.e., response consistency at that level.

Response consistency is an important requirement, but to exploit its usefulness in educational decisions it is necessary to postulate specific processes to account for that consistency. The nature of these constructs should, in turn, depend on the level of decisions based on scores. Such decisions range from individual-level decisions to decisions affecting a conglomerate of individuals (e.g., in program evaluation, statewide assessment, and national assessment). For decisions at the individual level psychological constructs are appropriate; however, as the data are aggregated and the focus of decisions changes from the individual to the aggregate, a different kind of construct becomes more relevant.

A potential source of constructs for validating achievement tests at the individual level is provided by the increasing number of investigations (e.g., Hunt, Lunnenborg, and Lewis, 1975; Carroll, 1980; Sternberg, 1980) that analyze test taking in terms of information-processing or cognitive constructs. The constructs identified by such research could be used for validating achievement tests for individual decisions. Such an approach would seem to blur the distinction between aptitude and achievement since it is likely that aptitude and achievement tests share many of the cognitive mechanisms that underlie test performance. However, the basic distinction between an achievement and an aptitude measure is not in terms of the psychological constructs that account for performance, but in terms of the substantive coverage of the test. For an achievement test, the rules that define the universe are dictated by a curriculum, whereas this is not the case for aptitude tests.

At a higher level of interpretation—say, from the perspective of a state-level department of education—interpretations of achievement test performance based on psychological constructs are not very useful. From the state's point of view interpretation of achievement must be made (in addition to individual-level constructs) in terms of constructs that are subject to manipulation through policy decisons. If, for example, the degree of availability of technology, such as educational computers, is seen to affect achievement at the district level, the state may decide to channel more funds toward the purchase of computers.

The interplay between kind of constructs and level of decision when the focus of decision is policy is illustrated in the controversy surrounding the conclusions of the Coleman report (Coleman et al., 1966) regarding the effect of schools on students. Of the many critiques of these data, the one by Madaus et al. (1980) is most concerned with measurement. Madaus et al. argued that the basic conclusions of the Coleman report, namely that home background is more influential than school effects, is probably invalid. First, the measure of "achievement" that was used was verbal ability, which they did not regard as a reasonable indicator of schooling outcomes. In other words, the dependent variable lacks construct validity for the intended application. They argued further that since verbal ability was used as a measure of achievement it is not surprising that home factors, rather than school factors, were found to be the more influential construct. The solution that Madaus et al. offers is to bring the content of the test closer to the curriculum and to measure other constructs explicitly, such as the quality of the interaction between the student and other students as well as school personnel. If it is found that such factors, which are in principle subject to manipulation, affect achievement, then we would have a basis for intelligent policy decisions. (See also Porter et al., 1980.)

The interplay between these dimensions at the student level is illustrated by Bejar and Weiss (1978). The purpose of the investigation was to develop a computer-assisted testing system for a large biology course. Decisions are therefore concerned with the student. The match between test content and curriculum was assured by the fact that the items were provided by the staff teaching the course. The model that was postulated to explain achievement included verbal ability as a determinant of achievement at two points in time. Verbal ability was found to be a significant influence on achievement. That is, other things being equal, a higher verbal ability (as measured by synonyms) contributes to higher achievement. Does it follow that a crash course in vocabulary development prior to the course will be useful in improving achievement?

Clearly, the answer is no. Even though verbal ability is a useful predictor of achievement, by itself it does not offer any guidelines as to how to improve achievement. To obtain those guidelines we need to account for performance in verbal ability in terms of information-processing variables (see Hunt et al., 1975). It is those information-processing constructs, rather than verbal ability as such, that are likely to be useful in accounting for differences in achievement and that will ultimately permit the design of optimal, individualized courses of instruction.

6. THE FUTURE OF ACHIEVEMENT TESTING

This paper has attempted to review recent developments relevant to the implementation of an achievement testing system. These developments were categorized into four areas: the creation of items, the psychometric foundation of the system, the administration procedure, and the interpretation and validation of test scores. This section discusses some of the future needs and expectations about achievement testing. Since achievement testing often has the dual purpose of providing information about the individual as well as aggregates of individuals, these final comments consider the role of achievement testing in the integration of instruction and assessment and the role of achievement testing in society.

Achievement at the Individual Level: Integrating Testing and Instruction

There is a growing consensus that tests must improve their usefulness for the individual. In the past, standardized achievement testing and instruction have been kept at a distance. Often a published test is given once or twice a year and has little if any impact on the course of instruction. The need to closely ally testing and instruction, indeed to integrate them, is beginning to be recognized. In a recent conference on testing sponsored by the National Institute of Education (Tyler and White, 1979), such an integration was viewed as very desirable. According to the chairpersons of the conference, there are four central elements in the integration of assessment and instruction: use of cognitive psychology, use of information-handling technology, involvement of teachers and subject-matter experts, and adaptability of the assessment-instruction package to practical applications.

Curiously absent from the requirements outlined by Tyler and White was any mention of the appropriate psychometric foundation for a system that integrates assessment and instruction. The absence of such mention, coupled with the emphasis on cognitive psychology, suggests a nonendorsement of criterion-referenced testing as the sole mechanism for achieving the desired integration of instruction and measurement.

An emphasis on cognitive psychology suggests a process-oriented interpretation of achievement. By contrast, criterion-referenced tests, minimum competency tests, and mastery testing emphasize *what* the student can or cannot do rather than *how* they do it. There is growing evidence of dissatisfaction with exclusively criterion-reference interpretation, even from the professionals whom such psychometric developments were designed to help. For example, Johnson and Pearson (1975) noted that commercially available criterion-referenced tests in reading or skills-monitoring systems, as they call them, suffer several weaknesses, including "psycholinguistic naivete." Moreover, advocates of criterion-referenced testing (e.g., Nitko, 1980; Hambleton et al., 1978) have begun to accept the role of construct validation in criterion-referenced testing. These trends suggest that the future of achievement testing will not be based solely on a behavioral interpretation of test scores.

There is little doubt that information-handling technology, including computers, will play a cruial role in the future of testing. The development of psychometric theory that makes adaptive testing possible, along with the ability to implement it with computers, is one of the most significant milestones in the history of psychometrics. It is almost certain that in the years ahead we will begin to see more application of computer-adaptive administration of tests. Indeed, it has been proposed that the testing battery used by the armed forces be administered by computer. Such a project has the potential to revolutionize testing practices just as the use of testing by the military did after World War I.

As noted by Bejar and Weiss (1978), however, the use of computers for the administration of achievement tests will simply improve testing efficiency. The challenge that lies ahead is how to improve the nature of achievement testing. There is no question that the computer will be involved, one way or another, in the solution of this challenge, but exactly how remains to be seen.

One possibility is the development of computer-based games. Many "educational" games exist currently, but their emphasis is on entertainment. It appears possible to develop games that are more directly linked to instruction. Work by Ira Goldstein (1980) at MIT is clearly headed in that direction. As other technologies—such as the videodisc, voice synthesizer, and recognition—are coupled with the computer, even more exotic games and simulations will be possible.

Clearly all of these possibilities raise questions for the direction and expansion of psychometric theory to support achievement testing in the years ahead. A key question is whether existing psychometric models, namely the L-T and R-S models discussed earlier, can provide the psychometric foundation needed by these developments. Research by some European psychometricians (e.g., Fischer and Foremann, 1982; Kempf and Hampapa, 1977; Spada, 1977) is extending the Rasch model to account for innovative testing situations. If these applications prove successful, the L-T model may continue to prove useful in future achievement applications. Nevertheless, it is likely that specialized measurement models will also be needed in some applications. As noted by Glaser (forthcoming), diagnostic testing is becoming increasingly important. The logic underlying diagnostic assessment appears to be different from that required by other measurement applications (Bejar, forthcoming a). Specifically, it seems to require close attention to the pattern of responses. The R-S model is oriented to the total score level and, in a sense, lumps together all response vectors that result in the same test score. The L-T model assigns a different score for every response pattern, but for diagnostic purposes what is needed is a means of assigning students to classes without necessarily ordering those classes, at least not with respect to overall achievement. The determination of a meaningful classification should involve a variety of professionals, including psychologists, teachers, test development experts, and psychometricians, in order to achieve an optimal blend of content and process considerations. As a result, it is likely that more attention will be given to individual items. That is, instead of viewing items as replications, items will be viewed as important entities.

Achievement Testing and Equal Educational Opportunity

In addition to being more useful as a means of individualizing instruction, the results of achievement testing will also be required to be more useful to society at large. The use of methodology to better society is not new. Campbell (1971) outlined the methodological needs of a utopia he called the "experimenting society." This society was committed to the solution of social problems. Since measurement of outcome variables provides the data on which decisions can most reasonably be made, it is clear that achievement testing will play a major role in the solution of educational problems—specifically the attainment of equal educational opportunity.

Equal educational opportunity has long been a national goal. As a result of many court cases, the operational definition of equal educational opportunity has been sharpened. That definition, in effect, is the collection of several statements of the following kind: "Students should not receive an inferior education because of factor X." Different court cases have addressed different factors. Thus, in Lau v. Nichols it was established that children should not receive an inferior education because of their linguistic background. In a methodological context the collection of these decisions postulate a model in which the outcome of education does not depend on those X factors.

It follows from this description that a relevant approach to the measurement of equal opportunity must postulate a statistical-psychometric model that estimates the relationship between as many X-factors as we can gather data on, and educational outcomes. The statistical component of the model is required in order to determine how well the proposed model holds and to guide modification of the model in the (likely) event that it does not fit the data as originally postulated. The statistical model is also needed to judge how well the model fits different subpopulations of interest.

The need for the psychometric model stems from the belief that achievement tests are possibly the best quantifiable indicator of the effect of schooling. The power of the psychometric devices as educational indicators has been eloquently demonstrated by the Scholastic Aptitude Test (SAT). For example, it was through the trends in SAT mean performance that we were first alerted to the so-called score decline and to the fact that "grade inflation" was a real phenomenon (Bejar and Blew, 1981).

The idea of monitoring equal educational opportunity by linking in a dynamic model determinants of achievement and educational outcome measures appears to be a novel one. The periodic survey conducted by the National Assessment of Educational Progress (NAEP), as well as those conducted by many state-wide testing programs, appear to be based on a descriptive rather than dynamic model of achievement. That is, they are content with comparing performances, often on a single item, across time and groups, rather than attempting to account for such differences. To the extent that such an accounting is possible, a dynamic model of achievement has a clear advantage over a descriptive model, for it can suggest mechanisms responsible for such differences and thus guide policy actions to minimize those differences. A model that incorporates these goals will be part of the new NAEP (Messick et al., 1983).

REFERENCES

AIRASIAN, P. W. and W. M. BART (1975) "Validating a priori instructional hierarchies." Journal of Educational Measurement 12: 163-173.

ANDERSEN, E. B. (1982) Latent Trait Models and Ability Parameter Estimation. Applied Psychological Measurement 6: 445-462.

ANDERSEN, E. B. (1977) "Sufficient statistics and latent trait models." Psychometrika 42: 69-81.

ANDERSEN, E. B. (1973) "A goodness of fit test for the Rasch model." Psychometrika 38: 123-140.

ANDERSEN, J., G. E. KEARNEY, and A. V. EVERETT (1968) "An evaluation of Rasch's structural model for test items." British Journal of Mathematical and Statistical Psychology 21: 231-238.

ANDRICH, D. (1978) A rating formulation for ordered response categories. Psychometrika 43: 561-573.

ANGOFF, W. H. (1971) "Scales, norms, and equivalent scores," in R. L. Thorndike (ed.) Educational Measurement. Washington, DC: American Council on Education.

BEJAR, I. I. (forthcoming a) "Educational diagnostic assessment." Journal of Educational Measurement.

—— (forthcoming b) "Speculations on the psychometrics of test design," in S. Whitely (ed.) Test Design: Contributions from Psychology, Education and Psychometrics. New York: Academic.

—— (forthcoming c) "Subject matter experts' assessment of item statistics." Applied Psychological Measurement.

—— (forthcoming d) "Assessment of partial knowledge, laten traits and computer-assisted testing." Educational and Psychological Measurement.

—— (1983) "Introduction to item response models and their assumptions," in R. K. Hambleton (ed.) ERIBC Monograph on Applications of Item Response Theory. Vancouver: Educational Research Institute of British Columbia.

—— (1980a) "A procedure for investigating the unidimensionality of achievement tests based on item parameter estimates." Journal of Educational Measurement 17: 283-296.

—— (1980b) "Biased assessment of program impact due to psychometric artifacts." Psychological Bulletin 87: 513-524.

—— (1977) "An application of the continuous response model to personality measurement." Applied Psychological Measurement 1: 509-522.

—— and E. O. BLEW (1981) "Grade inflation and the validity of the Scholastic Aptitude Test." American Educational Research Journal 18: 143-156.

BEJAR, I. I. and D. J. WEISS (1979) Computer Programs for Scoring Test Data with Item Characteristic Curve Models. Research Report 79-1; NTIS No. AD A067752. Minneapolis: Department of Psychology, University of Minnesota.

—— (1978) A Construct Validation of Adaptive Achievement Testing. Research Report 78-4. Minneapolis: Department of Psychology, University of Minnesota.

——— (1977) "Comparison of empirical differential option weighting scoring procedures as a function of inter-item correlation." Educational and Psychological Measurement 37: 335-340.

BEJAR, I. I. and M. WINGERSKY (1982) "A study of pre-equating based on item response theory." Applied Psychological Measurement 6: 309-325.

BEJAR, I. I., D. J. WEISS, and G. G. KINGSBURY (1977) Calibrating an Item Pool for the Adaptive Measurement of Achievement. Research Report 77-5. Minneapolis: Department of Psychology, University of Minnesota.

BENTLER, P. M. (1978) "The interdependence of theory, methodology, and empirical data: causal modeling as an approach to construct validation," in D. B. Kandel (ed.) Longitudinal Research on Drug Use. New York: Halstead.

BEREITER, C. (1963) "Some persisting dilemmas in the measurement of change," in C. W. Harris (ed.) Problems in Measuring Change. Madison: University of Wisconsin Press.

BERK, R. A. (1978) "The application of structural facet theory to achievement test construction." Educational Research Quarterly 3, 3: 62-72.

BETZ, N. E. and D. J. WEISS (1975) Empirical and Simulation Studies of Flexilevel Ability Testing. Research Report 75-3; NTIS No. AD AO13185. Minneapolis: Department of Psychology, University of Minnesota.

——— (1973) An Empirical Study of Computer-Administered Two-Stage Ability Testing. Research Report 73-4; NTIS No. AD 768993. Minneapolis: Department of Psychology, University of Minnesota.

BIRNBAUM, A. (1968) "Some latent trait models and their use in inferring an examinee's ability," in F. M. Lord and M. R. Novick, Statistical Theories of Mental Test Scores. Reading, MA: Addison-Wesley.

BLOCK, J. H. (1971) Mastery Learning: Theory and Practice. New York: Holt, Rinehart & Winston.

BLOOM, B. S. (1974) "Time and learning." American Psychologist 29: 682-688.

BOCK, R. D. (1976) "Basic issues in the measurement of change," in D.N.M. de Gruijter and L.J.T. van der Kamp (eds.) Advances in Psychological Measurement. London: John Wiley.

——— (1973) "Word and image: sources of the verbal and spatial factors in mental test scores." Psychometrika 38: 437-458.

——— (1972) "Estimating item parameters and latent ability when responses are scored in two or more nominal categories." Psychometrika 37: 29-52.

——— and M. AITKIN (1981) "Marginal maximum likelihood estimating item parameters: application of an EM algorithm." Psychometrika 46: 443-459.

BOCK, R. D. and M. L. LIEBERMAN (1970) "Fitting a response model for n dichotomously scored items." Psychometrika 35: 179-197.

BOCK, R. D. and R. J. MISLEVY (1982) Adaptive EAP estimation of ability in a microcomputer environment." Applied Psychological Measurement 6: 431-444.

BORMUTH, J. R. (1970) On the Theory of Achievement Test Items. Chicago: University of Chicago Press.

BRENNAN, R. L. (1983) Elements of Generalizability Theory. Iowa City: ACT Publications.

——— and M. T. KANE (1977) "Signal/noise ratios for domain-referenced test." Psychometrika 42: 609-626.

BURT, C. (1955) "Test reliability estimated by analysis of variance." British Journal of Statistical Psychology 8: 103-118.

CAMPBELL, D. T. (1971) "Methods for the experimenting society." Department of Psychology, Northwestern University.

CARROLL, J. B. (1980) "Measurements of abilities constructs," in Construct Validity in Psychological Measurement (Proceedings of a colloquium on theory and application in education and employment). Princeton, NJ: Educational Testing Service.

——— (1963) "A model of school learning." Teachers College Record, 64: 723-733.

CLIFF, N. (1975) "Complete orders from incomplete data: interactive ordering and tailored testing." Psychological Bulletin 82: 289-302.

——— R. CUDECK, and D. J. McCORMICK (1979) "Evaluation of implied orders as a basis for tailored testing with simulation data." Applied Psychological Measurement 3: 495-514.

COLEMAN, J. S. et al. (1966) Equality of Educational Opportunity. Washington, DC: U.S. Office of Education.

CRONBACH, L. J. (1970) "Review of On the Theory of Achievement Test Items, by J. R. Bormuth." Psychometrika 35: 509-511.

——— and H. AZUMA (1962) "Internal consistency reliability formulas applied to randomly sampled single-factor tests: an empirical comparison." Educational and Psychological Measurement 22: 645-665.

CRONBACH, L. J. and L. FURBY (1970) "How we should measure 'change'—or should we?" Psychological Bulletin 74: 68-80.

CRONBACH, L. J. and G. C. GLESER (1965) Psychological Tests and Personnel Decisions. Urbana: University of Illinois Press.

CRONBACH, L. J. and P. E. MEEHL (1955) "Construct validity in psychological tests." Psychological Bulletin 52: 281-302.

CRONBACH, L. J. and R. E. SNOW (1977) Aptitude and Instructional Methods. New York: Irvington.

CRONBACH, L. J., G. C. GLESER, H. NANDA, and N. RAJARATNAM (1972) The Dependability of Behavioral Measurements: Theory of Generalizability for Scores and Profiles. New York: John Wiley.

CRONBACH, L. J., N. RAJARATNAM, and G. C. GLESER (1963) "Theory of generalizability: a liberalization of reliability theory." British Journal of Statistical Psychology 16: 137-163.

DAVIS, C. E., J. HICKMAN and M. R. NOVICK (1973) A Primer on Decision Analysis for Individually Prescribed Instruction. Technical Bulletin 17. Iowa City: Research and Development Division, American College Testing Program.

De FINETTI, B. (1965) "Methods of discriminating levels of partial knowledge concerning a test item." British Journal of Mathematical and Statistical Psychology 13: 87-123.

De GRUIJTER, D.N.M. (1980) "A two-stage testing procedure," in L.J.T. van der Kamp et al. (eds.) Psychometrics for Educational Debates. New York: John Wiley.

DINERO, T. E. and E. HAERTEL (1977) "Applicability of the Rasch model with varying item discriminations." Applied Psychological Measurement 1: 581-592.

EBEL, R. L. (1979) "The case for norm-referenced measurements." Educational Researcher 7, 11: 3-5.

EDWARDS, A.W.F. (1972) Likelihood: An Account of the Statistical Concept of Likelihood and Its Application to Scientific Inference. London: Cambridge University Press.

EMRICK, J. A. (1971) "An evaluation model for mastery testing." Journal of Educational Measurement 8: 321-326.

FELDMAN, D. H. and W. MARKWALDER (1971) "Systematic scoring of ranked distractors for the assessment of Piagetian reasoning levels." Educational and Psychological Measurement 31: 347-362.

FERGUSON, G. A. (1942) "Item selection by the constant process." Psychometrika, 7: 19-29.

FINN, P. J. (1978) "Generating domain-referenced multiple-choice test items from prose passages." Presented at the annual meeting of the American Educational Research Association, Toronto.

FINN, P. J. (1975) "A question writing algorithm." Journal of Reading Behavior 4: 341-367.

FISCHER, G. H. (1980) "Some latent trait models for measuring change in qualitative observations," in D. J. Weiss (ed.) Proceedings of the 1979 Computerized Adaptive Testing Conference. Minneapolis: University of Minnesota.

——— and A. K. FORMANN (1982) "Some applications of logistic latent trait models with linear constraints on the parameters." Applied Psychological Measurement 6: 397-416.

FISCHER, G. H. and P. PENDL (1980) "Individualized testing on the basis of the dichotomous Rasch model," in L.J.T. van der Kamp et al., (eds.) Psychometrics for Educational Debates. New York: John Wiley.

GAGNÉ, R. M. (1975) "Observing the effects of learning." Educational Psychologist 11: 144-157.

——— and N. E. PARADISE (1961) "Abilities and learning sets in knowledge acquisition." Psychological Monographs 75 (14, Whole no. 508).

GAGNÉ, R. M., J. R. MAYOR, H. L. GARSTENS, and N. E. PARADISE (1962) "Factors in acquiring knowledge of a mathematical task." Psychological Monographs 76 (7, Whole no. 526).

GAGNÉ, R. M. et al. (1965) "University of Maryland Mathematics Project. Some factors in learning non-metric geometry." Monographs of the Society for Research in Child Development 30: 42-49.

GIALLUCA, K. A. and D. J. WEISS (1980) Effects of Immediate Knowledge of Results on Achievement Test Performance and Test Dimensionality. Research Report 80-1. Minneapolis: Department of Psychology, University of Minnesota.

GLASER, R. (forthcoming) "The future of testing: a research agenda for cognitive psychology and psychometrics." American Psychologist.

——— (1976) "Components of a psychology of instruction: toward a science of design." Review of Educational Research 46: 1-25.

——— and A. J. NITKO (1971) "Measurement in learning and instruction," in R. L.. Thorndike (ed.) Educational Measurement. Washington, DC: American Council on Education.

GLASS, G. V. (1978) "Standards and criteria." Journal of Educational Measurment 15: 237-261.

GOLDSTEIN, I. (1980) "Developing a computational representation of problem solving skills" in D. T. Tuma and F. Reif (eds.) Problem Solving and Education: Issues in Teaching and Research. Hillsdale, NJ: Erlbaum.

GREENO, J. G. (1978) "Review of Human Characteristics and School Learning, by B. Bloom." Journal of Educational Measurement 15: 67-76.

GUGEL, J. R., F. L. SCHMIDT, and V. W. URRY (1976) "Effectiveness of the ancillary estimation procedure," in C. L. Clark (ed.) Proceedings of the First Conference on

Computerized Adaptive Testing. PS-75-6, U. S. Civil Service Commission, Personnel Research and Development Center, Document 006-00940-a. Washington, DC: U. S. Government Printing Office.

GUILFORD, J. P. (1959) "The three faces of intellect." American Psychologist 14: 469-479.

GULLIKSEN, H. (1950) Theory of Mental Tests. New York: John Wiley.

GUTTMAN, L. (1980) "Integration of test desgin and analysis: status in 1979," in W. B. Schrader (ed.) Measuring Achievement: Progress Over a Decade. San Francisco: Jossey-Bass.

——— (1969) "Integration of test design and analysis," in Proceedings of the 1969 Invitational Conference on Testing Problems. Princeton, NJ: Educational Testing Service.

——— (1953) "A special review of Harold Gulliksen, Theory of Mental Tests." Psychometrika 18: 123-130.

——— and I. M. SCHLESINGER (1967) "Systematic constuction of distractors for ability and achievement test items." Educational and Psychological Measurement 27: 569-580.

HALADYNA, T. and G. ROID (1978) "A comparison of several multiple-choice linguistic-based item writing algorithms." Presented at the annual meeting of the American Educational Research Association, Toronto.

HAMBLETON, R. K. (1983) "Application of item response models to criterion referenced assessment." Applied Psychological Measurement 7: 733-744.

——— (1979) "Latent trait models and applications," in R. E. Traub (ed.) New Directions for Testing and Measurement: Analysis of Test Data. San Francisco: Jossey-Bass.

——— and L. L. COOK (1977) "Latent trait models and their use in the analysis of educational test data." Journal of Educational Measurement 14: 76-96.

HAMBLETON, R. K. and L. MURRAY (1983) "Some goodness of fit investigations for item response models," in R. K. Hambleton (ed.) ERIBC Monograph on Applications of Item Response Theory. Vancouver: Education Research Institute of British Columbia.

HAMBLETON, R. K. and M. R. NOVICK (1973) "Toward an integration of theory and method for criterion-referenced tests." Journal of Educational Measurement 10: 159-170.

HAMBLETON, R. K., H. SWAMINATHAN, J. ALGINA, and D. B. COULSON (1978) "Criterion-referenced testing and measurement: a review of technical issues and developments." Review of Educational Research 48: 1-47.

HAMBLETON, R. K., H. SWAMINATHAN, L. L. COOK, D. R. EIGNOR, and J. A. GIFFORD (1978) "Developments in latent trait theory: models, technical issues and applications." Review of Educational Research 48: 467-510.

HARRIS, C. W. [ed.] (1963) Problems in Measuring Change. Madison: University of Wisconsin Press.

——— A. PASTOROK, and R. R. WILCOX (1977) Achievement Test Items-Methods of Study. Los Angeles: Center for the Study of Evaluation, University of California.

HARRIS, D. A. and R. J. PENNELL (1977) Simulated and Empirical Studies of Flexilevel Testing in Air Force Technical Training Courses. Report AFHRL-TR-77-51. Brooks Air Force Base, TX: Human Resources Laboratory.

HIVELY, W. (1974) "Introduction to domain referenced testing." Educational Technology 14: 5-9.

HOYT, C. (1941) "Test reliability estimated by analysis of variance." Psychometrika 6: 153-160.

HUNT, E., C. LUNNENBORG, and J. LEWIS (1975) "What does it mean to be high verbal?" Cognitive Psychology 1: 194-227.

HUYHN, H. (1976) "Statistical considerations of mastery scores." Psychometrika 42: 65-79.

INDOW, T. and SAMEJIMA, F. (1966) On the Results Obtained by the Absolute Scaling Model and the Lord Model in the Field of Intelligence. Yokohama: Psychological Laboratory, Hiyoshi Campus, Keio University.

JOHNSON, D. and P. D. PEARSON (1975) "Skills management systems: a critique." The Reading Teacher (May): 757-764.

KANE, M. T. and R. L. BRENNAN (1980) "Agreement coefficients as indices of dependability for domain references tests." Applied Psychological Measurement 4: 105-126.

KELLEY, T. L. (1947) Fundamentals of Statistics. Cambridge, MA: Harvard University Press.

KEMPF, W. F. and P. HAMPAPA (1977) "Conditional inference for the dynamic test model," in W. F. Kempf and B. H. Repp (eds.) Mathematical Models for Social Psychology. New York: John Wiley.

KENDALL, M. G. and A. STUART (1961) The Advanced Theory of Statistics, vol. 2. New York: Hafner.

KINGSBURY, G. G. and D. J. WEISS (1979) Effect of Point-In-Time in Instruction on the Measurement of Achievement. Research Report 79-4. Minneapolis: Department of Psychology, University of Minnesota.

KOHLBERG, L. (1969) "Stage and sequence: the cognitive developmental approach to socialization," in D. A. Goslin (ed.) Handbook of SocializationTheory and Research. Chicago: Rand McNally.

KREITZBERG, C. B., M. STOCKING, and L. SWANSON (1978) "Computerized adaptive testing." Computers and Education 2: 319-329.

LAWLEY, D. N. (1943) "On problems connected with item selection and test construction." Proceedings of the Royal Society of Edinburgh 61: 273-287.

LAZARSFELD, P. F. (1959) "Latent structure analysis," in S. Koch (ed.) Psychology: A Study of Science, vol. 3. New York: McGraw-Hill.

LEWIS, C., M. M. WANG, and M. R. NOVICK (1975) "Marginal distributions for the estimation of proportions in groups." Psychometrika 1: 63-75.

LIEBERMAN, M. (1973) "Psychometric analysis of developmental stage data." Presented at the annual meeting of the American Psychological Association, Montreal.

LINDGREN, B. W. (1971) Elements of Decision Theory. New York: Macmillan.

LINDLEY, D. V. and L. D. PHILLIPS (1976) "Influence for a Bernoulli process (a Bayesian view)." The American Statistician 30: 112-118.

LINDLEY, D. V. and A.F.M. SMITH (1972) "Bayes estimates for the linear model." Journal of the Royal Statistical Society 34: 1-41.

LINDQUIST, E. F. (1953) Design and Analysis of Experiments in Psychology and Education. Boston: Houghton Mifflin.

LINN, R. L. and J. A. SLINDE (1977) "The determination of the significance of change between pre- and posttesting periods." Review of Educational Research 47: 121-150.

LIVINGSTON, S. A. (1972) "Criterion-referenced applications of classical test theory." Journal of Educational Measurement 9: 13-26.

LOEVINGER, J. (1965) "Person and population as psychometric concepts." Psychological Review 72: 143-155.

LONG, J., J. SCHAFFRAN and T. KELLOGG (1977) "Effects of out-of-level survey testing on reading achievement scores of Title I ESEA students." Journal of Educational Measurement 14: 203-213.

LORD, F. M. (forthcoming) "Small n justifies Rasch methods," in D. J. Weiss (ed.) New Horizons in Testing. New York: Academic.

—— (1980a) Application of Item Response Theory to Practical Testing Problems. Hillsdale, NJ: Erlbaum.

—— (1980b) "Somehow and which for practical tailored testing," in L.J.T. van der Kamp et al. (eds.) Psychometric for Educational Debates. New York: John Wiley.

—— (1977a) "Some item analysis and test theory for a system of computer-assisted test construction for individualized instruction." Applied Psychological Measurement 1: 447-456.

—— (1977b) "A broad range tailored test of verbal ability." Applied Psychological Measurement 1: 95-100.

—— (1977c) "Practical applications of item characteristic curve theory." Journal of Educational Measurement 14: 117-138.

—— (1975) Evaluation with Artificial Data of a Procedure for Estimating Ability and Item Characteristic Curve Parameter. ETS RB 75-33. Princeton, NJ: Educational Testing Service.

—— (1974) "The relative efficiency of two tests as a function of ability level." Psychometrika 39: 351-358.

—— (1971) "A theoretical study of two-stage testing." Psychometrika 36: 227-242.

—— (1952) "A theory of test scores." Psychometrika Monograph, no. 7.

—— and M. R. NOVICK (1968) Statistical Theories of Mental Test Scores. Reading, MA: Addison-Wesley.

McBRIDE, J. R. (1979) Adaptive Mental Testing: The State of the Art. Technical Report 4237. Alexandria, VA: Research Institute for the Behavioral and Social Sciences.

McCREADY, G. B. (1975) "The structure of domain hierarchy found within a domain referenced testing system." Educational and Psychological Measurement 35: 583-598.

McKINLEY, R. L., and M. D. RECKASE (1980) A Successful Application of Latent Trait Theory to Tailored Achievement. Research Report No. 80-1. Columbia: Educational Psychology Department, University of Missouri.

MADAUS, G. F., P. W. AIRASIAN, and J. KELLAGHAN (1980) School Effectiveness: A Reassessment of the Evidence. New York: McGraw-Hill.

MARCO, G., N. PETERSEN, and E. STEWART (1980) "A test of the adequacy of curvilinear score equating models," in D. J. Weiss (ed.) Proceedings of the 1979 Computerized Adaptive Testing Conference. Minneapolis: University of Minnesota.

MASTERS, G. N. (1982) "A Rasch model for partial credit scoring." Psychometrika 47: 149-174.

MESSICK, S. (1981) "Constructs and their vicissitudes in educational and psychological measurement." Psychological Bulletin 89: 575-588.

—— (1980) "Test validity and the ethics of assessment." American Psychologist 35: 1012-1027.

—— (1975) "The standard problem: meaning and values in measurement and evaluation." American Psychologist 30: 955-966.

—— B. BEATON, and F. M. LORD (1983) National Assessment of Educational Progress Reconsidered: A New Design for a New Area. Princeton, NJ: Center for the Assessment of Educational Progress, Educational Testing Service.

MILLMAN, J. (1974) "Criterion-referenced measurement," in W. J. Popham (ed.) Evaluation in Education. Berkeley, CA: McCutchan.

MOLENAAR, I. N. (1983) "Some improved diagnostics for failure of the Rasch model. Psychometrika 48: 49-72.

NEDELSKY, L. (1954) "Absolute grading standards for objective tests." Educational and Psychological Measurement 14: 3-19.

NITKO, A. J. (1980) "Distinguishing the many varieties of criterion referenced tests." Review of Educational Research 50: 461-486.

NOVICK, M. R. and P. H. JACKSON (1974) Statistical Methods for Educational and Psychological Research. New York: McGraw-Hill.

OLIVIER, P. (1974) "An evaluation of the self-scoring flexilevel testing model." Ph.D. dissertation, Florida State University.

OSBURN, H. G. (1968) "Item sampling for achievement testing." Educational and Psychological Measurement 28: 95-104.

OSTERLIND, S. J. (1983) Test Item Bias. Sage University Paper series on Quantitative Application in the Social Sciences, 07-030. Beverly Hills, CA: Sage.

OWEN, D. (1983) "Breakdown at merit control: the last days of Educational Testing Service." Harper's, (March).

OWEN, R. J. (1975) "A Bayesian sequential procedure for quantal response in the context of adaptive testing." Journal of the American Statistical Association 70: 351-356.

POPHAM, W. J. (1978) "The case for criterion referenced measurements." Educational Researcher 7, 11: 6-10.

——— and T. R. HUSEK (1969) "Implications of criterion-referenced measurement." Journal of Educational Measurement 6: 1-9.

PORTER, A. C., W. H. SCHMIDT, R. E. FLODEN, and D. J. FREEMAN (1980) Impact on What?: The Importance of Content Covered. College of Education, Michigan State University, February.

RAGOSA, D., D. BRANDT and M. ZIMOWSKI (1982) "A growth curve approach to the measurement of change." Psychological Bulletin 92: 726-748.

RASCH, G. (1960) Probabilistic Models for Some Intelligence and Attainment Tests. Copenhagen: Nielson & Lydiche.

RECKASE, M. D. (1977) Ability Estimation and Item Calibration Using One and Three Parameter Logistic Models: A Comparative Study. Research Report 77-1. Columbia: Department of Educational Psychology, University of Missouri.

RENTZ, R. R. and C. C. RENTZ (1979) "Does the Rasch model really work? A discussion for practitioners." Measurement in Education 10, 2: 1-11.

RINDSKOPF, D. (1983) "A general framework for using latent class analysis to test hierarchical learning models." Psychometrika 48: 85-97.

ROID, G. and T. HALADYNA (1982) A Technology for Test-Item Writing. New York: Academic.

——— (1980) "The emergence of item writing technology." Review of Educational Research 50: 293-314.

——— (1978) "A comparison of objective-based and modified-Bormuth item writing techniques." Educational and Psychological Measurement 38: 19-28.

ROSNER, J. (1975) "Testing for teaching in an adaptive educational environment," in W. Hively and M. C. Reynolds (eds.) Domain Referenced Testing in Special Education. Reston, A: Council for Exceptional Children.

SAMEJIMA, F. (1977) "Effects of individual optimization in setting the boundaries of dichotomous items on the accuracy of estimation." Applied Psychological Measurement 1: 77-94.

——— (1974) "Normal ogive model on the continuous response level in the multidimensional latent space." Psychometrika 39: 111-121.

———— (1973) "Homogeneous case of the continuous response model." Psychometrika 38: 203-219.

———— (1972) "A general model for free response data." Psychometrika Monograph, no. 18.

———— (1969) "Estimation of latent ability using a response pattern of graded scores." Psychometrika Monograph, no. 17.

SANATHANAN, L. (1980) "Latent structure estimation for assessing gain in ability," in D. J. Weiss (ed.) Proceedings of the 1979 Computerized Adaptive Testing Conference. Minneapolis: University of Minnesota.

SCANDURA, J. M. (1977) "Structural approach to instructional problems." American Psychologist 32: 33-53.

SEGUIN, S. P. (1976) "An exploratory study of the efficiency of the flexilevel testing procedure." Ph.D. dissertation, University of Toronto.

SHOEMAKER, D. M. (1975) "Toward a framework for achievement testing." Review of Educational Research 48: 127-141.

———— and H. G. OSBURN (1970) "A simulation model for achievement testing." Educational and Psychological Measurement 30: 267-272.

SHUFORD, E. H., A. ALBERT, and H. F. MASSENGILL (1966) "Admissible probability measurement procedures." Psychometrika 31: 125-145.

SIROTNICK, R. (1974) "An introduction for matrix sampling for the practitioner," in W. J. Popham (ed.) Evaluation in Education: Current Applications. Berkeley, CA: McCutchan.

SLINDE, J. A. and R. LINN (1979) "The Rasch model objective measurement, equating, and robustness." Applied Psychological Measurement 16: 437-452.

———— (1978) "An exploration of the adequacy of the Rasch model for the problem of vertical equating." Journal of Educational Measurement 15: 23-35.

SPADA, H. (1977) "Logistic models of learning and thought," in H. Spada and W. H. Kempf (eds.) Structural Models of Thinking and Learning. Bern: Huber. (Also Fort Lee, NJ: Update.)

STERNBERG, R. J. (1980) "The construct validity of aptitude tests: an information-processing assessment," in Construct Validity in Psychological Measurement (Proceedings of a colloquium on theory and application in education and employment). Princeton, NJ: Educational Testing Service.

SUBKOVIAK, M. J. (1976) "Estimating reliability from a single administration of a criterion referenced test." Journal of Educational Measurement 13: 265-276.

SWAMINATHAN, H. (1983) "Parameter estimation in item response models," in R. K. Hambleton (ed.) ERIBC Monograph on Applications of Item Response Theory. Vancouver: Education Research Institute of British Columbia.

———— R. K. HAMBLETON, and J. ALGINA (1974) "Reliability of criterion referenced tests: a decision theoretic formulation." Journal of Educational Measurement 11: 263-267.

SYMPSON, J. B. (1978) "A model for testing with multidimensional items," in D. J. Weiss (ed.) Proceedings of the 1977 Computerized Adaptive Testing Conference. Minneapolis: University of Minnesota.

———— (1977) "Estimation of latent trait status in adaptive testing procedures," in D. J. Weiss (ed.) Applications of Computerized Adaptive Testing. Research Report 77-1, AD 0A038114. Minneapolis: University of Minnesota.

TENOPYR, M. L. (1977) "Content-construct confusion." Personnel Psychology 30: 47-54.

THISSEN, D. (1982) "Marginal maximum likelihood estimation for the one-parameter logistic model." Psychometrika 47: 175-186.

——— (1976) "Information in wrong responses to Raven's Progressive Matrices." Journal of Educational Measurement 13: 201-214.

TRAUB, R. E. (1983) "A priori considerations in choosing an item response model," in R. K. Hambleton (ed.) ERIBC Monograph on Applications of Item Response Theory. Vancouver: Educational Research Institute of British Columbia.

——— and R. G. WOLFE (1981) "Latent trait theories and the assessment of educational achievement," in D. C. Berliner (ed.) Review of Research in Education, vol. 9. Washington, DC: American Educational Research Association.

TRAVERS, R.M.W. (1980) "Taxonomies of educational objectives and theories of classification." Educational Evaluation and Policy Analysis 2: 5-24.

TRYON, R. C. (1957) "Reliability and behavior domain validity: reformulation and historical critique." Psychological Bulletin 54: 229-249.

TUCKER, L. R. (1946) "Maximum validity of a test with equivalent items." Psychometrika 11: 1-13.

TYLER, R. W. and S. H. WHITE [Chairmen] (1979) Testing, Teaching, and Learning: Report of a Conference on Research on Testing. Washington, DC: National Institute of Education.

VALE, C. D. (1977) Adaptive Testing and the Problem of Classification. Research Report 77-1. Minneapolis: Department of Psychology, University of Minnesota.

Van den WOLLENBERG, A. L. (1982) "Two new test statistics for the Rasch model. Psychometrika 47: 123-140.

WAINER, H., A. MORGAN, and J. E. GUSTAFSSON (1980) "A review of estimation procedures for the Rasch model with an eye toward longish tests." Journal of Educational Statistics 5: 35-64.

WALLER, M. I. (1980) "An objective procedure for comparing the one, two and three-parameter logistic latent trait model." Presented at the annual convention of the American Educational Research Association, Boston.

WANG, M. W. and J. C. STANLEY (1970) "Differential weighting: a review of methods and empirical studies." Review of Educational Research 40: 663-705.

WANG, M. W., M. R. NOVICK, G. L. ISAACS, and D. OZENNE (1977) "A Bayesian data analysis system for the evaluation of social programs." Journal of the American Statistical Association 72: 711-722.

WEISS, D. J. (1982) "Improving measuring quality and efficiency with adaptive testing." Applied Psychological Measurement 6, 4: 473-492.

——— (1974) Strategies of Adaptive Ability Measurement. Research Report 74-5. Minneapolis: Department of Psychology, University of Minnesota.

——— (1973) The stratified Adaptive Computerized Ability Test. Research Report 73-3. Minneapolis: Department of Psychology, University of Minnesota.

WELLINGTON, R. (1976) "Extending generalized symetric means to arbitrary matrix sampling designs." Psychometrika 1: 375-384.

WESSMAN, A. G. (1971) "Writing the test item," in R. L. Thorndike (ed.) Educational Measurement. Washington, DC: American Council in Education.

WHITE, R. T. (1973) "Research into learning hierarchies." Review of Educational Research 43: 361-375.

WHITELEY, S. E. (1980) "Multicomponent latent trait model for ability tests." Psychometrika 45: 479-494.

——— (1977) "Models, meaning and misunderstanding: some issues in applying Rasch's theory." Journal of Educational Measurement 14: 217-235.

——— R. V. DAWIS (1976) "The influence of text context on item difficulty." Educational and Psychological Measurement 36: 329-337.

——— (1974) "The nature of objectivity with the Rasch model." Journal of Educational Measurement 11: 3, 163-178.

WILCOX, R. R. (1979) "Achievement tests and latent structure models." British Journal of Mathematical and Statistical Psychology 32: 61-71.

WITTROCK, M. C. and A. A. LUMSDAINE (1977) "Instructional psychology," in M. R. Rosenzweig and L. W. Porter (eds.) Annual Review of Psychology, vol. 28. Palo Alto, CA: Annual Reviews Inc.

WOOD, R. (1976) "Trait measurement and item banks," In D.N.M. de Gruijter and L.J.T. van der Kamp (eds.) Advances in Psychological and Educational Measurement. New York: John Wiley.

——— (1973) "Response-contingent testing." Review of Educational Research 43: 529-544.

——— and L. S. SKURNIK (1969) Item Banking: A Method for Producing School-Based Examinations and Nationally Comparable Grades. London: National Foundation for Educational Research in England & Wales.

WRIGHT, B. D. (1977) "Solving measurement problems with the Rasch model." Journal of Educational Measurement 14: 97-116.

YEN, W. M. (1980) "The extent, causes and importance of context effects on item parameters for the latent trait models." Journal of Educational Measurement 17: 297-312.

ISAAC I. BEJAR earned a Ph.D. in psychology from the University of Minnesota in 1975 and held a postdoctoral research fellowship at Northwestern University. He holds the title of Research Scientist at Educational Testing Service, where he performs research on the integration of psychometric theory, cognitive psychology, and computer technology. Among his other professional activities, he has served as consultant to bilingual programs in several states. He is also a member of the editorial board of Applied Psychological Measurement.

Quantitative Applications in the Social Sciences

(a Sage University Papers Series)

$6.00 each

SAGE PUBLICATIONS, INC.
P.O. BOX 5024
BEVERLY HILLS, CALIFORNIA 90210

Place
Stamp
here